São Paulo

Alex & Gardênia Robinson

Credits

Footprint credits
Editorial and production: Nicola Gibbs
Maps: Kevin Feeney

Publisher: Patrick Dawson
Managing Editor: Felicity Laughton
Advertising: Elizabeth Taylor
Sales and marketing: Kirsty Holmes

Photography credits
Front cover: Alex Robinson
Back cover: Alex Robinson

Printed in Great Britain by Alphaset,
Surbiton, Surrey

Every effort has been made to ensure that
the facts in this guidebook are accurate.
However, travellers should still obtain advice
from consulates, airlines, etc, about travel
and visa requirements before travelling.
The authors and publishers cannot accept
responsibility for any loss, injury or
inconvenience however caused.

The content of Footprint *Focus São Paulo*
has been taken directly from Footprint's
Brazil Handbook, which was researched and
written by Alex and Gardênia Robinson.

Publishing information
Footprint *Focus São Paulo*
2nd edition
© Footprint Handbooks Ltd
February 2014

ISBN: 978 1 909268 81 4
CIP DATA: A catalogue record for this book
is available from the British Library

® Footprint Handbooks and the Footprint
mark are a registered trademark of
Footprint Handbooks Ltd

Published by Footprint
6 Riverside Court
Lower Bristol Road
Bath BA2 3DZ, UK
T +44 (0)1225 469141
F +44 (0)1225 469461
footprinttravelguides.com

Distributed in the USA by Globe Pequot
Press, Guilford, Connecticut

Contents

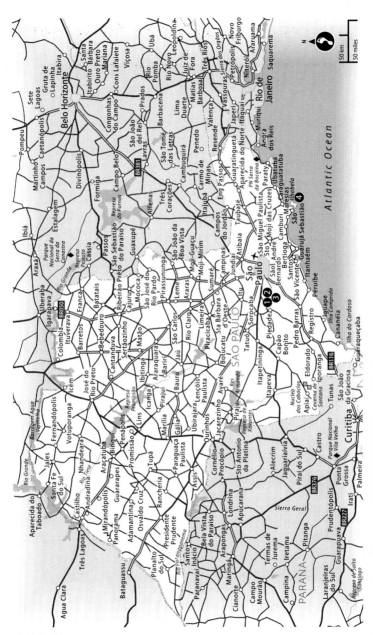

São Paulo is as famous for its ugliness as Rio is for its beauty. But while Rio looks marvellous from a distance and less than perfect close to, São Paulo is the opposite. Restaurants, shops, hotels and nightlife here are infinitely better than in Rio. And, while wandering and browsing in plush neighbourhoods such as Jardins, it is even possible to forget that few cities in the world have quite so much relentless concrete punctuated with quite so few green spaces; or have rivers quite so disgracefully polluted as the Tietê. Marlene Dietrich perhaps summed it up when she said – "Rio is a beauty – but São Paulo; ah ... São Paulo is a city."

Indeed, São Paulo is more than a city. It is also a state a little larger than the UK; and while most of its interior is dull agricultural hinterland, its coast is magnificent; just as beautiful as Rio de Janeiro's but far less visited by international tourists. The northern beaches are long and glorious and pounded by some of South America's finest surf. Brazil's largest island, which is every bit as pristine and romantic as Ilha Grande, lies a short boat ride off shore. The beaches further south are less beautiful but far wilder; behind them, stretching into the neighbouring state of Paraná, are the largest expanses of primary forest on Brazil's Atlantic coast.

Planning your trip

Best time to visit São Paulo

The best time to visit São Paulo is from April to June, and August to October. Business visitors should avoid mid-December to the end of February, when it is hot and people are on holiday. In these months, hotels, beaches and transport tend to be very crowded. July is a school holiday month. Conditions during the winter (May to September) are like those of a Mediterranean autumn. Summer conditions are tropical, although temperatures rarely reach 40°C. The heaviest rain is from November to March. A small area of the Serra do Mar, between Santos and São Paulo, receives more than 2 m of rainfall annual and the downpour has been harnessed to generate electricity. Humidity is relatively high, particularly along the coast. The luminosity is also very high, and sunglasses are advisable.

Getting to São Paulo

Air
Flights into Brazil generally land at **Cumbica International Airport** at Guarulhos (often used as an alternative name) in São Paulo (see page 19). The airport has direct connections with the rest of South and Central America, the USA, Canada, Mexico, Europe and Asia, and indirect connections with Australasia via Buenos Aires, Santiago or Los Angeles. Prices are cheapest in October/November and after Carnaval in February, and at their highest in the European summer and the Brazilian high seasons (generally 15 December to 15 January, the Thursday before Carnaval to the Saturday after Carnaval, and 15 June to 15 August). Departure tax is usually included in the cost of the ticket.

Air passes
TAM and GOL offer a 21-day **Brazil Airpass**, which is valid on any TAM destination within Brazil. The price varies according to the number of flights taken and the international airline used to arrive in Brazil. They can only be bought outside Brazil. Rates vary depending on the season. Children pay a discounted rate; those under three pay 10% of the adult rate. Some of the carriers operate a blackout period between 15 December and 15 January.

Baggage allowance
Airlines will only allow a certain weight of luggage without a surcharge; for Brazil this is usually two items of 32 kg but may be as low as 20 kg; with two items of hand luggage weighing up to 10 kg in total. UK airport staff can refuse to load bags weighing more than 30 kg. Baggage allowances are higher in business and first class. Weight limits for internal flights are often lower, usually 20 kg. In all cases it is best to enquire beforehand.

Transport in São Paulo

Public transport in Brazil is very efficient, but distances are huge. Most visitors will find themselves travelling by buses and planes. Train routes are practically non-existent, car hire is expensive and hitchhiking not advisable. Taxis vary widely in quality and price but are easy to come by and safe when taken from a *posto de taxis* (taxi rank).

Don't miss...

1 **Fine art in MASP**, page 35.
2 **Oscar Niemeyer buildings in São Paulo**, page 41.
3 **São Paulo restaurants and nightlife**, page 51 and 56
4 **Beaches and waterfalls on Ilhabela**, page 74.

Numbers relate to the map on page 4.

Air

Because of the size of the country, flying is often the most practical option and internal air services are highly developed. All state capitals and larger cities are linked with each other with services several times a day, and all national airlines offer excellent service. Recent deregulation of the airlines has greatly reduced prices on some routes and low-cost airlines offer fares that can often be as cheap as travelling by bus (when booked through the internet). Paying with an international credit card is not always possible online; but it is usually possible to buy an online ticket through a hotel, agency or willing friend without surcharge. Many of the smaller airlines go in and out of business sporadically. **Avianca** ⓘ *www.avianca.com.br*, **Azul** ⓘ *www.voeazul.com.br*, **GOL** ⓘ *www.voegol.com.br*, **TAM** ⓘ *www.tam.com.br*, and **TRIP** ⓘ *www.voetrip.com.br*, operate the most extensive routes.

Road

The best paved highways are heavily concentrated in the southeast, but roads serving the interior are being improved to all-weather status and many are paved. Most main roads between principal cities are paved. Some are narrow and therefore dangerous; many are in poor condition.

Bus There are three standards of bus: *Comum*, or *Convencional*, are quite slow, not very comfortable and fill up quickly; *Executivo* are more expensive, comfortable (many have reclining seats), and don't stop en route to pick up passengers so are safer; *leito* (literally 'bed') run at night between the main centres, offering reclining seats with leg rests, toilets, and sometimes refreshments, at double the normal fare. For journeys over 100 km, most buses have chemical toilets (bring toilet paper). Air conditioning can make buses cold at night, so take a jumper; on some services blankets are supplied.

Buses stop fairly frequently (every two to four hours) at *postos* for snacks. Bus stations for interstate services and other long-distance routes are called *rodoviárias*. They are frequently outside the city centres and offer snack bars, lavatories, left luggage, local bus services and information centres. Buy bus tickets at *rodoviárias* (most now take credit cards), not from travel agents who add on surcharges. Reliable bus information is hard to come by, other than from companies themselves. Buses usually arrive and depart in very good time. Many town buses have turnstiles, which can be inconvenient if you are carrying a large pack. Urban buses normally serve local airports.

Car hire Renting a car in Brazil is expensive: the cheapest rate for unlimited mileage for a small car is about US$65 per day. These costs can be more than halved by reserving a car over the internet through one of the larger international companies such as **Europcar**

(www.europcar.co.uk) or **Avis** (www.avis.co.uk). The minimum age for renting a car is 21 and it's essential to have a credit card. Companies operate under the terms *aluguel de automóveis* or *auto-locadores*. Check exactly what the company's insurance policy covers. In many cases it will not cover major accidents or 'natural' damage (eg flooding). Ask if extra cover is available. Sometimes using a credit card automatically includes insurance. Beware of being billed for scratches that were on the vehicle before you hired it.

Taxi Rates vary from city to city, but are consistent within each city. At the outset, make sure the meter is cleared and shows 'tariff 1', except (usually) from 2300-0600, Sunday, and in December when '2' is permitted. Check that the meter is working; if not, fix the price in advance. **Radio taxis** cost about 50% more but cheating is less likely. Taxis outside larger hotels usually cost more. If you are seriously cheated, note the number of the taxi and insist on a signed bill; threatening to take it to the police can work. **Mototaxis** are much cheaper, but many are unlicensed and there have been a number of robberies of passengers.

Where to stay in São Paulo

There is a good range of accommodation options in Brazil. An *albergue* or hostel offers the cheapest option. These have dormitory beds and single and double rooms. Many are part of the IYHA ① *www.iyha.org*. Hostel World ① *www.hostelworld.com*; **Hostel Bookers** ① *www.hostelbookers.com*; and **Hostel.com** ① *www.hostel.com*, are useful portals. **Hostel Trail Latin America** ① *T0131-2080007 (UK), www.hosteltrail.com*, managed from their hostel in Popayan, is an online network of hotels and tour companies in South America. A *pensão* is either a cheap guesthouse or a household that rents out some rooms.

Pousadas
A *pousada* is either a bed-and-breakfast, often small and family-run, or a sophisticated and often charming small hotel. A *hotel* is as it is anywhere else in the world, operating according to the international star system, although five-star hotels are not price controlled and hotels in any category are not always of the standard of their star equivalent in the USA, Canada or Europe. Many of the older hotels can be cheaper than hostels. Usually accommodation prices include a breakfast of rolls, ham, cheese, cakes and fruit with coffee and juice; there is no reduction if you don't eat it. Rooms vary too. Normally an *apartamento* is a room with separate living and sleeping areas and sometimes cooking facilities. A *quarto* is a standard room; *com banheiro* is en suite; and *sem banheiro* is with shared bathroom. Finally there are the *motels*. These should not be confused with their US counterpart: motels are used by guests not intending to sleep; there is no stigma attached and they usually offer good value (the rate for a full night is called the '*pernoite*'), however the decor can be a little garish.

It's a good idea to book accommodation in advance in small towns that are popular at weekends with city dwellers (eg near São Paulo), and it's essential to book at peak times. **Hidden Pousadas Brazil** ① *www.hiddenpousadasbrazil.com*, offers a range of the best *pousadas* around the country.

Luxury accommodation
Much of the best private accommodation can be booked through operators. **Angatu**, www.angatu.com, offers the best private homes together with bespoke trips. **Matuete**, www.matuete.com, has a range of luxurious properties and tours throughout Brazil.

Price codes

Hotels

$$$$	over US$150	**$$$**	US$66-150
$$	US$30-65	**$**	under US$30

Price of a double room in high season, including taxes.

Restaurants

$$$	over US$12	**$$**	US$7-12	**$**	under US$7

Prices for a two-course meal for one person, excluding drinks or service charge.

Camping

Those with an international camping card pay only half the rate of a non-member at **Camping Clube do Brasil** sites ⓘ *www.campingclube.com.br*. Membership of the club itself is expensive: US$90 for six months. The club has 43 sites in 13 states and 80,000 members. It may be difficult to get into some Camping Clube campsites during high season (January to February). Private campsites charge about US$10-15 per person. For those on a very low budget and in isolated areas where there is no campsite available, it's usually possible to stay at service stations. They have shower facilities, watchmen and food; some have dormitories. There are also various municipal sites. Campsites tend to be some distance from public transport routes and are better suited to people with their own car. Wild camping is generally difficult and dangerous. Never camp at the side of a road; this is very risky.

Homestays

Staying with a local family is an excellent way to become integrated quickly into a city and companies try to match guests to their hosts. **Cama e Café** ⓘ *www.camaecafe.com. br*, organizes homestays in a number of cities around Brazil. **Couch surfing** ⓘ *www. couchsurfing.com*, offers a free, backpacker alternative.

Quality hotel associations

The better international hotel associations have members in Brazil. These include: **Small Luxury Hotels of the World** ⓘ *www.slh.com*; the **Leading Hotels of the World** ⓘ *www. lhw.com*; the **Leading Small Hotels of the World** ⓘ *www.leadingsmallhotelsoftheworld. com*; **Great Small Hotels** ⓘ *www.greatsmallhotels.com*; and the French group **Relais et Chateaux** ⓘ *www.relaischateaux.com*, which also includes restaurants.

The Brazilian equivalent of these associations are **Hidden Pousadas Brazil** ⓘ *www. hiddenpousadasbrazil.com*, and their associate, the **Roteiros de Charme** ⓘ *www. roteirosdecharme.com.br*. Membership of these groups pretty much guarantees quality, but it is by no means comprehensive.

Online travel agencies (OTAs)

Services like **www.tripadvisor.com** and OTAs associated with them – such as **www.hotels. com**, **www.expedia.com** and **www.venere.com**, are well worth using for both reviews and for booking ahead. Hotels booked through an OTA can be up to 50% cheaper than the rack rate. Similar sites operate for hostels include the Hostelling International site, **www. hihostels.com**, **www.hostelbookers.com**, **www.hostels.com** and **www.hostelworld.com**.

Food and drink in São Paulo

Food

While Brazil has some of the best fine dining restaurants in Latin America, everyday Brazilian cuisine – particularly in the southeast can be stolid. Mains are generally heavy, meaty and unspiced. Desserts are often very sweet. In São Paulo, a heady mix of international immigrants has resulted in some unusual fusion cooking and exquisite variations on French, Japanese, Portuguese, Arabic and Italian traditional techniques and dishes and the regional cooking can be a delight. However, at times it can be a struggle to find interesting food. The Brazilian staple meal generally consists of a cut of fried or barbecued meat, chicken or fish accompanied by rice, black or South American broad beans and an unseasoned salad of lettuce, grated carrot, tomato and beetroot. Condiments consist of weak chilli sauce, olive oil, salt and pepper and vinegar.

The national dish is a greasy campfire stew called *feijoada*, made by throwing jerked beef, smoked sausage, tongue and salt pork into a pot with lots of fat and beans and stewing it for hours. The resulting stew is sprinkled with fried *farofa* (manioc flour) and served with *couve* (kale) and slices of orange. The meal is washed down with *cachaça* (sugarcane rum). Most restaurants serve the *feijoada completa* for Saturday lunch (up until about 1630). Come with a very empty stomach.

Brazil's other national dish is mixed grilled meat or *churrasco*, served in vast portions off the spit by legions of rushing waiters, and accompanied by a buffet of salads, beans and mashed vegetables. *Churrascos* are served in *churrascarias* or *rodízios*. The meat is generally excellent, especially in the best *churascarias*, and the portions are unlimited, offering good value for camel-stomached carnivores able to eat one meal a day.

In remembrance of Portugal, but bizarrely for a tropical country replete with fish, Brazil is also the world's largest consumer of cod, pulled from the cold north Atlantic, salted and served in watery slabs or little balls as *bacalhau* (an appetizer/bar snack) or *petisco*. Other national *petiscos* include *kibe* (a deep-fried or baked mince with onion, mint and flour), *coxinha* (deep-fried chicken or meat in dough), *empadas* (baked puff-pastry patties with prawns, chicken, heart of palm or meat), and *tortas* (little pies with the same ingredients). When served in bakeries, *padarias* or snack bars these are collectively referred to as *salgadinhos* (savouries).

Eating cheaply

The cheapest dish is the *prato feito* or *sortido*, an excellent-value set menu usually comprising meat/chicken/fish, beans, rice, chips and salad. The *prato comercial* is similar but rather better and a bit more expensive. Portions are usually large enough for two and come with two plates. If you are on your own, you could ask for an *embalagem* (doggy bag) or a *marmita* (takeaway) and offer it to a person with no food (many Brazilians do). Many restaurants serve *comida por kilo* buffets where you serve yourself and pay for the weight of food on your plate. This is generally good value and is a good option for vegetarians. *Lanchonetes* and *padarias* (diners and bakeries) are good for cheap eats, usually serving *prato feitos*, *salgadinhos*, excellent juices and other snacks.

The main meal is usually taken in the middle of the day; cheap restaurants tend not to be open in the evening.

Drink

The national liquor is *cachaça* (also known as *pinga*), which is made from sugar-cane, and ranging from cheap supermarket and service-station fire-water, to boutique distillery and connoisseur labels from the interior of Minas Gerais. Mixed with fruit juice, sugar and crushed ice, *cachaça* becomes the principal element in a *batida*, a refreshing but deceptively powerful drink. Served with pulped lime or other fruit, mountains of sugar and smashed ice it becomes the world's favourite party cocktail, caipirinha. A less potent caipirinha made with vodka is called a *caipiroska* and with sake a *saikirinha* or *caipisake*.

Some genuine Scotch whisky brands are bottled in Brazil. They are far cheaper even than duty free; Teacher's is the best. Locally made and cheap gin, vermouth and campari are pretty much as good as their US and European counterparts.

Wine is becoming increasingly popular, with good-value Portuguese and Argentine bottles and some reasonable national table wines such as Château d'Argent, Château Duvalier, Almadén, Dreher, Preciosa and more respectable Bernard Taillan, Marjolet from Cabernet grapes, and the Moselle-type white Zahringer. A new *adega* tends to start off well, but the quality gradually deteriorates with time; many vintners have switched to American Concorde grapes, producing a rougher wine. Greville Brut champagne-style sparkling wine is inexpensive and very drinkable.

Brazil is the third most important wine producer in South America. The wine industry is mainly concentrated in the south of the country where the conditions are most suitable, with over 90% of wine produced in Rio Grande do Sul. There are also vineyards in Pernambuco. There are some interesting sparkling wines in the Italian spumante style (the best is Casa Valduga Brut Premium Sparkling Wine), and Brazil produces still wines using many international and imported varieties. None are distinguished – these are drinkable table wines at best. At worst they are plonk of the Blue Nun variety. The best bottle of red is probably the Boscato Reserva Cabernet Sauvignon. But it's expensive (at around US$20 a bottle); you'll get far higher quality and better value buying Portuguese, Argentine or Chilean wines in Brazil.

Brazilian beer is generally lager, served ice-cold. Draught beer is called *chope* or *chopp* (after the German Schoppen, and pronounced 'shoppi'). There are various national brands of bottled beers, which include Brahma, Skol, Cerpa, Antartica and the best Itaipava and Bohemia. There are black beers too, notably Xingu. They tend to be sweet. The best beer is from the German breweries in Rio Grande do Sul and is available only there.

Brazil's myriad fruits are used to make fruit juices or *sucos*, which come in a delicious variety, unrivalled anywhere in the world. *Açaí acerola, caju* (cashew), *pitanga, goiaba* (guava), *genipapo, graviola* (chirimoya), *maracujá* (passion fruit), *sapoti, umbu* and *tamarindo* are a few of the best. *Vitaminas* are thick fruit or vegetable drinks with milk. *Caldo de cana* is sugar-cane juice, sometimes mixed with ice. *Água de côco* or *côco verde* is coconut water served straight from a chilled, fresh, green coconut. The best known of many local soft drinks is *guaraná*, which is a very popular carbonated fruit drink, completely unrelated to the Amazon nut. The best variety is *guaraná Antarctica*. Coffee is ubiquitous and good tea entirely absent.

Essentials A-Z

Accident and emergency

Ambulance T192. **Police** T190. If robbed or attacked, contact the tourist police. If you need to claim on insurance, make sure you get a police report.

Electricity

Generally 110 V 60 cycles AC, but in some cities and areas 220 V 60 cycles AC is used. European and US 2-pin plugs and sockets.

Embassies and consulates

For embassies and consulates of Brazil, see www.embassiesabroad.com.

Health → *Hospitals/medical services are listed in the Directory sections of each chapter.*

See your GP or travel clinic at least 6 weeks before departure for general advice on travel risks and vaccinations. Make sure you have sufficient medical travel insurance, get a dental check, know your own blood group and, if you suffer a long-term condition such as diabetes or epilepsy, obtain a **Medic Alert** bracelet (www.medicalalert.co.uk).

Vaccinations and anti-malarials

Confirm that your primary courses and boosters are up to date. It is advisable to vaccinate against polio, tetanus, typhoid, hepatitis A and, for more remote areas, rabies. Yellow fever vaccination is obligatory for most areas. Cholera, diptheria and hepatitis B vaccinations are sometimes advised. Seek specialist advice on the best antimalarials to take before you leave.

Health risks

The major risks posed in the region are those caused by insect disease carriers such as mosquitoes and sandflies. The key parasitic and viral diseases are malaria, South American trypanosomiasis (Chagas disease) and dengue fever. Be aware that you are always at risk from these diseases. **Malaria** is a danger throughout the lowland tropics and coastal regions. **Dengue fever** (which is currently rife in Rio de Janeiro state) is particularly hard to protect against as the mosquitoes can bite throughout the day as well as night (unlike those that carry malaria); try to wear clothes that cover arms and legs and also use effective mosquito repellent. Mosquito nets dipped in permethrin provide a good physical and chemical barrier at night. **Chagas disease** is spread by faeces of the triatomine, or assassin bugs, whereas sandflies spread a disease of the skin called **leishmaniasis**.

Some form of **diarrhoea** or intestinal upset is almost inevitable, the standard advice is always to wash your hands before eating and to be careful with drinking water and ice; if you have any doubts about the water then boil it or filter and treat it. In a restaurant buy bottled water or ask where the water has come from. Food can also pose a problem, be wary of salads if you don't know if it has been washed or not.

There is a constant threat of **tuberculosis** (TB) and although the BCG vaccine is available, it is still not guaranteed protection. It is best to avoid unpasteurized dairy products and try not to let people cough and splutter all over you.

Another risk, especially to campers and people with small children, is that of the **hanta virus**, which is carried by some forest and riverine rodents. Symptoms are a flu-like illness which can lead to complications. Try to avoid rodent-infested areas, especially close contact with droppings.

Money
Currency → £1 = 3.9; €1 = 3.3; US$1 = R$2.4 (Feb 2014).

The unit of currency is the **real**, R$ (plural **reais**). Any amount of foreign currency and 'a reasonable sum' in reais can be taken in, but sums over US$10,000 must be declared. Residents may only take out the equivalent of US$4000. Notes in circulation are: 100, 50, 10, 5 and 1 real; coins: 1 real, 50, 25, 10, 5 and 1 centavo. **Note** The exchange rate fluctuates – check regularly.

Costs of travelling
Brazil is more expensive than other countries in South America. As a very rough guide, prices are about two-thirds those of Western Europe and a little cheaper than rural USA.

Hostel beds are usually around US$15. Budget hotels with few frills have rooms for as little as US$30, and you should have no difficulty finding a double room costing US$45 wherever you are. Rooms are often pretty much the same price whether 1 or 2 people are staying. Eating is generally inexpensive, especially in *padarias* or *comida por kilo* (pay by weight) restaurants, which offer a wide range of food (salads, meat, pasta, vegetarian). Expect to pay around US$6 to eat your fill in a good-value restaurant. Although bus travel is cheap by US or European standards, because of the long distances, costs can soon mount up. Internal flights prices have come down dramatically in the last couple of years and some routes work out cheaper than taking a bus – especially if booking through the internet. Prices vary regionally. Ipanema is almost twice as expensive as rural Bahia.

ATMs
ATMs, or cash machines, are common in Brazil. As well as being the most convenient way of withdrawing money, they frequently offer the best available rates of exchange.

They are usually closed after 2130 in large cities. There are 2 international ATM acceptance systems, **Plus** and **Cirrus**. Many issuers of debit and credit cards are linked to one, or both (eg Visa is Plus, MasterCard is Cirrus). **Bradesco** and HSBC are the 2 main banks offering this service. **Red Banco 24 Horas** kiosks advertise that they take a long list of credit cards in their ATMs, including MasterCard and Amex, but international cards cannot always be used; the same is true of **Banco do Brasil**.

Advise your bank before leaving, as cards are usually stopped in Brazil without prior warning. Find out before you leave what international functionality your card has. Check if your bank or credit card company imposes handling charges. Internet banking is useful for monitoring your account or transferring funds. Do not rely on one card, in case of loss. If you do lose a card, immediately contact the 24-hr helpline of the issuer in your home country (keep this number in a safe place).

Exchange
Banks in major cities will change cash and traveller's cheques (TCs). If you keep the official exchange slips, you may convert back into foreign currency up to 50% of the amount you exchanged. The parallel market, found in travel agencies, exchange houses and among hotel staff, often offers marginally better rates than the banks but commissions can be very high. Many banks may only change US$300 minimum in cash, US$500 in TCs. Rates for TCs are usually far lower than for cash, they are harder to change and a very heavy commission may be charged.

Credit cards
Credit cards are widely used, although often they are not usable in the most unlikely of places, such as tour operators. Diners Club, **MasterCard**, **Visa** and **Amex** are useful. Cash

advances on credit cards will only be paid in reais at the tourist rate, incurring at least a 1.5% commission. Banks in remote places may refuse to give a cash advance: try asking for the *gerente* (manager).

Opening hours

Generally Mon-Fri 0900-1800; closed for lunch sometime between 1130 and 1400. **Shops** Also open on Sat until 1230 or 1300. **Government offices** Mon-Fri 1100-1800. **Banks** Mon-Fri 1000-1600 or 1630; closed at weekends.

Safety

Although Brazil's big cities suffer high rates of violent crime, this is mostly confined to the *favelas* (slums) where poverty and drugs are the main cause. Visitors should not enter *favelas* except when accompanied by workers for NGOs, tour groups or other people who know the local residents well and are accepted by the community. Otherwise they may be targets of muggings by armed gangs who show short shrift to those who resist them. Mugging can take place anywhere. Travel light after dark with few valuables (avoid wearing jewellery and use a cheap, plastic, digital watch). Ask hotel staff where is and isn't safe; crime is patchy in Brazilian cities.

If the worst does happen and you are threatened, don't panic, and hand over your valuables. Do not resist, and report the crime to the local tourist police later. It is extremely rare for a tourist to be hurt during a robbery in Brazil. Being aware of the dangers, acting confidently and using your common sense will reduce many of the risks.

Photocopy your passport, air ticket and other documents, make a record of traveller's cheque and credit card numbers. Keep them separately from the originals and leave another set of records at home. Keep all documents secure; hide your main cash supply in different places or under your clothes. Extra pockets sewn inside shirts and trousers, money belts (best worn below the waist), neck or leg pouches and elasticated support bandages for keeping money above the elbow or below the knee have been repeatedly recommended.

All border areas should be regarded with some caution because of smuggling activities. Violence over land ownership in parts of the interior have resulted in a 'Wild West' atmosphere in some towns, which should therefore be passed through quickly. Red-light districts should also be given a wide berth as there are reports of drinks being drugged with a substance popularly known as 'good night Cinderella'. This leaves the victim easily amenable to having their possessions stolen, or worse.

Avoiding cons

Never trust anyone telling sob stories or offering 'safe rooms', and when looking for a hotel, always choose the room yourself. Be wary of 'plain-clothes policemen'; insist on seeing identification and on going to the police station by main roads. Do not hand over your identification (or money) until you are at the station. On no account take them directly back to your hotel. Be even more suspicious if they seek confirmation of their status from a passer-by.

Hotel security

Hotel safe deposits are generally, but not always, secure. If you cannot get a receipt for valuables in a hotel safe, you can seal the contents in a plastic bag and sign across the seal. Always keep an inventory of what you have deposited. If you don't trust the hotel, lock everything in your pack and secure it in your room when you go out. If you lose valuables, report to the police and note details of the report for insurance purposes. Be sure to be present whenever your credit card is used.

Police

There are several types of police: **Polícia Federal**, civilian dressed, who handle all federal law duties, including immigration. A subdivision is the **Polícia Federal Rodoviária**, uniformed, who are the traffic police on federal highways. **Polícia Militar** are the uniformed, street police force, under the control of the state governor, handling all state laws. They are not the same as the Armed Forces' internal police. **Polícia Civil**, also state controlled, handle local laws and investigations. They are usually in civilian dress, unless in the traffic division. In cities, the *prefeitura* controls the **Guarda Municipal**, who handle security. **Tourist police** operate in places with a strong tourist presence. In case of difficulty, visitors should seek out tourist police in the first instance.

Public transport

When you have all your luggage with you at a bus or railway station, be especially careful and carry any shoulder bags in front of you. To be extra safe, take a taxi between the airport/bus station/railway station and hotel, keep your bags with you and pay only when you and your luggage are outside; avoid night buses and arriving at your destination at night.

Sexual assault

If you are the victim of a sexual assault, you are advised firstly to contact a doctor (this can be your home doctor). You will need tests to determine whether you have contracted any STDs; you may also need advice on emergency contraception. You should contact your embassy, where consular staff will be very willing to help.

Telephone → *Country code: +55.*

Ringing: equal tones with long pauses. Engaged: equal tones, equal pauses.

Making a phone call in Brazil can be confusing. It is necessary to dial a 2-digit telephone company code prior to the area code for all calls. Phone numbers are now printed in this way: 0XX11 (0 for a national call, XX for the code of the phone company chosen (eg 31 for Telemar) followed by '11' for São Paulo, for example, and the 8-digit number of the subscriber. The same is true for international calls where 00 is followed by the operator code and then the country code and number.

Time

Brazil has 4 time zones: Brazilian standard time is GMT-3. Clocks move forward 1 hr in summer for approximately 5 months (usually between Oct and Feb or Mar), but times of change vary.

Tipping

Tipping is not usual, but always appreciated as staff are often paid a pittance. In restaurants, add 10% of the bill if no service charge is included; cloakroom attendants deserve a small tip; porters have fixed charges but often receive tips as well; unofficial car parkers on city streets should be tipped R$2.

Tourist information

The **Ministério do Turismo**, Esplanada dos Ministérios, Bloco U, 2nd and 3rd floors, Brasília, www.turismo.gov.br or www.braziltour.com, is in charge of tourism in Brazil and has information in many languages. **Embratur**, the Brazilian Institute of Tourism, is at the same address, and is in charge of promoting tourism abroad. For information and phone numbers for your country visit www.braziltour.com. Local tourist information bureaux are not usually helpful for information on cheap hotels – they generally just dish out pamphlets. Telephone directories (not Rio) contain good street maps.

Other good sources of information are: **LATA**, www.lata.org. The Latin American Travel Association, with useful country information and listings of all UK operators specializing in Latin America. Also has up-to-date information on public safety, health, weather, travel costs, economics and politics highlighted for each nation. Wide selection of Latin American maps available, as well as individual travel planning assistance. **South American Explorers**, formerly the **South American Explorers Club**, 126 Indina Creek Rd, Ithaca, NY 14850, T607-277 0488, www.samexplo.org. A non-profit educational organization functioning primarily as an information network for South America.

National parks

National parks are run by the Brazilian institute of environmental protection, **Ibama**, SCEN Trecho 2, Av L-4 Norte, Edif Sede de Ibama, CEP 70818-900, Brasília, DF, T061-3316 1212, www.ibama.gov. br. For information, contact **Linha Verde**, T0800-618080, linhaverde.sede@ibama. gov.br. National parks are open to visitors, usually with a permit from Ibama. See also the **Ministério do Meio Ambiente** website, www.mma.gov.br.

Visas and immigration

Visas are not required for stays of up to 90 days by tourists from Andorra, Argentina, Austria, Bahamas, Barbados, Belgium, Bolivia, Chile, Colombia, Costa Rica, Denmark, Ecuador, Finland, France, Germany, Greece, Iceland, Ireland, Italy, Liechtenstein, Luxembourg, Malaysia, Monaco, Morocco, Namibia, the Netherlands, Norway, Paraguay, Peru, Philippines, Portugal, San Marino, South Africa, Spain, Suriname, Sweden, Switzerland, Thailand, Trinidad and Tobago, United Kingdom, Uruguay, the Vatican and Venezuela. For them, only the following documents are required at the port of disembarkation: a passport valid for at least 6 months (or *cédula de identidad* for nationals of Argentina, Chile, Paraguay and Uruguay); and a return or onward ticket, or adequate proof that you can purchase your return fare, subject to no remuneration being received in Brazil and no legally binding or contractual documents being signed. Venezuelan passport holders can stay for 60 days on filling in a form at the border.

Citizens of the USA, Canada, Australia, New Zealand and other countries not mentioned above, and anyone wanting to stay longer than 180 days, *must* get a visa before arrival, which may, if you ask, be granted for multiple entry. US citizens must be fingerprinted on entry to Brazil. Visa fees vary from country to country, so apply to the Brazilian consulate in your home country. The consular fee in the USA is US$55. Students planning to study in Brazil or employees of foreign companies can apply for a 1- or 2-year visa. 2 copies of the application form, 2 photos, a letter from the sponsoring company or educational institution in Brazil, a police form showing no criminal convictions and a fee of around US$80 is required.

Identification

You must always carry identification when in Brazil. Take a photocopy of the personal details in your passport, plus your Brazilian immigration stamp, and leave your passport in the hotel safe deposit. This photocopy, when authorized in a *cartório*, US$1, is a legitimate copy of your documents. Be prepared, however, to present the originals when travelling in sensitive border areas. Always keep an independent record of your passport details. Also register with your consulate to expedite document replacement if yours gets lost or stolen.

Warning Do not lose the entry/exit permit they give you when you enter Brazil. Leaving the country without it, you may have to pay up to US$100 per person. It is suggested that you photocopy this form and have it authenticated at a *cartório*, US$1, in case of loss or theft.

Weights and measures

Metric.

Contents

Footprint features

At a glance

☻ **Getting around** Metrô, city bus and long-distance bus. Taxi is the only option for some journeys. Car hire recommended for the coast.

♨ **Time required** 2-3 days for the city; preferably over a weekend for nightlife. 5-7 days to visit the city and parts of the state.

☼ **Weather** Warm and wet in summer (Oct-Mar) on the coast; drier inland with blue skies. Cool in winter (Apr-Sep) with blue skies. Temperatures can drop to below 10°C during a cold front.

✖ **When not to go** Jan-Feb is very wet.

São Paulo

São Paulo city

São Paulo is vast and can feel intimidating on first arrival. But this is a city of separate neighbourhoods, only a few of which are interesting for visitors, and once you have your base it is easy to navigate. São Paulo is the commercial capital of Brazil and the locus for this continent-sized country's culture. Those who are prepared to spend time (and money) here, and who get to know Paulistanos, are seldom disappointed. Nowhere in Brazil is better for concerts, clubs, theatre, ballet, classical music, restaurants and beautifully designed hotels. And nowhere in Brazil has so much of Brazil contained within it. Brazilians from all over the country make São Paulo their home and have left their cultural mark on the city, together with immigrants from the world over, most notably from Italy and Japan.

Arriving in São Paulo city

→ For listings, see pages 48-68. Phone code: 011.
Population: 18-20 million. Altitude: 850 m.

Getting there

Air São Paulo is Brazil's main international entry point and its domestic transport hub. There are three airports, the main international airport at Guarulhos in the suburbs, Congonhas airport near the city centre (which is principally domestic) and Campinas airport in the commuter town of Campinas some 95 km from São Paulo.

Nearly all international flights and many of the cheapest internal flights arrive at **Guarulhos Airport** ① *Guarulhos, 25 km northeast of the city, T011-2445 2945, www.infraero.gov.br,* officially known as **Cumbica**. There are plenty of banks and money changers in the arrivals hall, open daily 0800-2200, and cafés, restaurants and gift shops on the second floor and arrivals lobby. There is a post office on the third floor of Asa A. Tourist information, including city and regional city maps and copies of the entertainment section from the Folha de São Paulo newspaper with current listings, is available from **Secretaria de Esportes e Turismo (SET)** ① *ground floor of both terminals, Mon-Fri 0730-2200, Sat, Sun and holidays 0900-2100.*

Airport taxis charge US$65 to the centre and operate on a ticket system: go to the second booth on leaving the terminal and book a co-op taxi at the Taxi Comum counter; these are the best value. **Guarucoop** ① *T011-6440 7070, 24 hrs, www.aeroportoguarulhos.net,* is a leading, safe radio taxi company operating from the airport. The following **Emtu buses** ① *www.emtu. sp.gov.br/aeroporto,* run every 30-45 minutes (depending on the bus line) from Guarulhos between 0545 and 2215, to the following locations: **Nos 257** and **299** – Guarulhos to Metrô Tatuape (for the red line and connections to the centre), US$2; **No 258** for Congonhas airport via Avenida 23 de Maio and Avenida Rubem Berta, US$15; **No 259** for the Praça da República via Luz and Avenida Tiradentes, US$15; **No 316** for the principal hotels around Paulista and Jardins via Avenida Paulista, Rua Haddock Lobo and Rua Augusta, US$15; **No 437** for Itaím and Avenida Brigadeiro Faria Lima in the new business district, via Avenida Nove de Julho and Avenida Presidente Juscelino Kubitschek; and **No 472** for the Barra Funda Rodoviária and *metrô* station via the Rodoviária Tiete. A full timetable for each line with precise leaving times is listed on the website. **Airport Bus Service Pássaro Marron** ① *T0800-285 3047, www. airportbusservice.com.br,* also run buses between the airport, the city centre, *rodoviária,* Congonhas airport, Avenida Paulista and Jardins hotels, Avenida Faria Lima, Metrô Tatuape, *rodoviária* Tietê and the Praca da República. Buses leave every 10 minutes from 0500-0200 costing US$12.50, children under five free. All are air conditioned and a free paper and bottle of water is provided for the journey. They also run a service directly from the airport to Ubatuba and São Sebastião (for Ilhabela). Full details of this and other services are listed on their website. The company have waiting rooms in terminals 1 and 2 at Guarulhos – look for their distinctive red and blue logo or ask at the tour information desk if you can't find the lounge.

Flights with the Brazilian franchise of the US budget airline, **Azul** ① *www.voeazul.com. br,* have begun to run from **Viracopos Airport** in the city of **Campinas** just under 100 km from São Paulo, which the company cheekily calls São Paulo Campinas airport. Fares are very competitive and the company runs a bus connection between Campinas and São Paulo which connects with the flights. Azul buses leave from Terminal Barra Funda and Shopping Eldorado (Estação CPTM Hebraica Rebouças) around every 30 minutes – see the website for details.

The domestic airport, **Congonhas** ① *Av Washington Luiz, 7 km south of the centre, 5 km from Jardins, T011-5090 9000, www.aeroportocongonhas.net,* is used for the Rio–São Paulo shuttle and other domestic services. A taxi to the city centre or Jardins costs about US$30.

Bus Buses in São Paulo are operated by **SP Trans** ⓘ *www.sptrans.com.br*, who have an excellent bus route planner on their website. The system is fairly self-explanatory even for non-Portuguese speakers – with boxes allowing you to select a point of departure (*de*)

1 São Paulo Metrô and CPTM urban rail

➜ **São Paulo maps**
1 São Paulo Metrô & CPTM, page 20
2 São Paulo, page 26
3 São Paulo centre & Bela Vista, page 28
4 Avenida Paulista & Jardins, page 36

◆ **METRÔ**
metro.sp.gov.br
0800 770 7726

◆ **CPTM**
cptm.sp.gov.br
0800 055 0121

and destination (*para*). It also enables you to plan using a combination of bus, *metrô* and urban light railway (*trem*). Google maps mark São Paulo bus stops and numbers. Right clicking on the number shows the bus route and time and there is a search facility for planning routes. There is a flat fee of US$1.20 for any bus ride – payable to a conductor

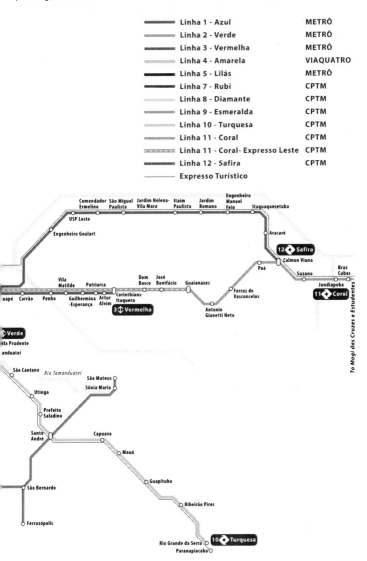

	Linha 1 - Azul	METRÔ
	Linha 2 - Verde	METRÔ
	Linha 3 - Vermelha	METRÔ
	Linha 4 - Amarela	VIAQUATRO
	Linha 5 - Lilás	METRÔ
	Linha 7 - Rubi	CPTM
	Linha 8 - Diamante	CPTM
	Linha 9 - Esmeralda	CPTM
	Linha 10 - Turquesa	CPTM
	Linha 11 - Coral	CPTM
	Linha 11 - Coral- Expresso Leste	CPTM
	Linha 12 - Safira	CPTM
	Expresso Turístico	

sitting behind a turnstile in the bus. The conductors are helpful in indicating where to hop on and off. Buses are marked with street names indicating their routes, but these routes can be confusing for visitors and services slow due to frequent traffic jams. However, buses are safe, clean and only crowded at peak hours (0700-0900 and 1700-1830). Maps of the bus and *metrô* system are available at depots, eg Anhangabaú.

Metrô and the CPTM Urban light railway The best and cheapest way to get around São Paulo is on the excellent **metrô system** ① *daily 0500-2400, www.metro.sp.gov.br, with a clear journey planner and information in Portuguese and English*, which is clean, safe, cheap and efficient. It is integrated with the overground CPTM light railway. São Paulo's was the first *metrô* in Brazil, beginning operations in 1975. It now has five main lines.

The **CPTM** (Companhia Paulista de Trens Metropolitanos) ① *www.cptm.sp.gov.br*, is an urban light railway which serves to extend the *metrô* along the margins of the Tietê and Pinheiros rivers and to the outer city suburbs. There are six lines, which are colour-coded like the *metrô*.

Taxi Taxis in São Paulo are white with a green light on the roof. They display their tariffs in the window (starting at US$5) and have meters. Ordinary taxis are hailed on the street or more safely at taxi stations (*postos*), which are never more than five minutes' walk away anywhere in the city. Hotels, restaurants and some venues will call a taxi on request – either from a *posto* or a taxi driver himself. Radio taxis are more expensive but less hassle.

Orientation
The **Centro Histórico** lies at the heart of the city and, although it is undergoing renovation, it remains a place to visit rather than to stay. Most of the historical buildings and former beauty are long gone, but its pedestrianized streets are fascinating and gritty, with lively markets and a cluster of interesting sights lost in the concrete and cobbles. For a birds' eye view of the city, head to the lookout platform at the top of the **Edifício Itália** (see page 32) or **Banespa tower** (see page 31), preferably at dusk. The old commercial district or **Triângulo**, bounded by Ruas Direita, 15 de Novembro, São Bento and Praça Antônio Prado (and nowadays spreading right to the Praça da República), lies sprawling in front of you in ranks of skyscraper banks, offices, shops and remnant historical buildings. This is one of São Paulo's three commercial centres.

Another lies immediately southwest of the Centro Histórico along the city's grandest and most photographed skyscraper-lined street, **Avenida Paulista**. The Museo de Arte de São Paulo (MASP), the best art gallery in the southern hemisphere, is here. Just to the north of Avenida Paulista is the neighbourhood of **Consolação**; centred on tawdry Rua Augusta but undergoing a renaissance, it is at the cutting edge of the city's underground live music and nightlife scene. South of Avenida Paulista are the **Jardins**, São Paulo's most affluent inner-city neighbourhoods, with elegant little streets hiding Latin America's best restaurants and designer clothing boutiques, together with swish hotels and serviced apartments (with a handful of budget options nearby). A short taxi ride away, **Pinheiros** and **Vila Madalena** offer an equally cool but more alternative shopping and nightlife scene, with lively clubs and a florescence of young designer boutiques and art galleries. There are a handful of cheaper places to stay here too.

Next to Jardins, 5 km south of the centre, the **Parque do Ibirapuera** is the inner city's largest green space, with running tracks, a lake and live concerts. Like Pampulha in Belo

Arriving late at night

São Paulo's international airport, Cumbica in Guarulhos, has 24-hour facilities (for food, banking and of course taxis) in case you arrive late at night or in the early hours of the morning. It is a long drive from the airport to the city and the a/c bus to Praça da República does not operate between 0200 and 0500 and the service to Avenida Paulista does not run from 2315 to 0645. A taxi to the centre of the city will cost around US$65.

Congonhas Airport, which is connected to most of Brazil's major cities, is in the city centre. Although there are no 24-hour services there are hotels across the road from the terminal (via the footbridge) and most areas in and around the centre are a maximum of US$30 taxi ride away.

Horizonte, the park is a repository of historically important Oscar Niemeyer buildings, many of which are home to interesting museums. The adjoining neighbourhoods of **Vila Mariana** and **Paraíso** have a few hotel options and great live music at SESC Vila Mariana.

Situated between Ibirapuera and the river, **Itaim**, **Moema** and **Vila Olímpia** are among the nightlife centres of São Paulo with a wealth of street-side bars, ultra-chic designer restaurants and European-style dance clubs. Hotels tend to be expensive as these areas border São Paulo's third and newest commercial centre, lying on and around Avenida Brigadeiro Faria Lima and Avenida Luís Carlos Berrini, which stretches into the suburb of **Brooklin**. Many of the better business hotels are in this area.

Tourist information

There are tourist information booths with English-speaking staff in international and domestic arrivals (on the ground floor near the exit) at **Cumbica Airport** (Guarulhos) ⓘ *www.aeroportoguarulhos.net*. There are also tourist information booths in the **bus station** and in the following locations throughout the city: **Praça da Luz** ⓘ *in front of the Pinacoteca cafe, daily 0900-1800*; **Avenida São João** ⓘ *Av São João 473, Mon-Fri 0900-1800*; **Avenida Paulista** ⓘ *Parque Trianon, T011-3251 0970, Sun-Fri 0900-1800*; and **Avenida Brig Faria Lima** ⓘ *opposite the Iguatemi shopping centre, T011-3211 1277, Mon-Fri 0900-1800*. An excellent map is available free at these offices.

Websites The websites www.guiasp.com.br and www.vejasp.abril.com.br have comprehensive entertainment listings

Background

The history of São Paulo state and São Paulo city were much the same from the arrival of the Europeans until the coffee boom transformed the region's economic and political landscape. According to John Hemming, author of *Red Gold* – an authoritative history of indigenous Brazil in colonial times – there were approximately 196,000 indigenous inhabitants living in what is now São Paulo state at the time of conquest. Today their numbers have been vastly diminished though of the few who survived, some live in villages within metropolitan São Paulo itself and can be seen selling handicrafts in the centre.

The first official settlement in the state was at São Vicente on the coast, near today's port of Santos. It was founded in 1532 by Martim Afonso de Sousa, who had been sent by

King João III to drive the French from Brazilian waters, explore the coast and lay claim to all the lands apportioned to Portugal under the Treaty of Tordesillas.

In 1554, two Jesuit priests from São Vicente founded São Paulo as a *colégio* (a combined mission and school) on the site of the present Pátio de Colégio in the Centro Histórico. The Jesuits chose to settle inland because they wanted to distance themselves from the civil authority, which was based in Bahia and along the coast. Moreover, the plateau provided better access to the indigenous population who they hoped to convert to Catholicism. Pioneers seeking to found farms followed in the Jesuits' wake and as the need for workers on these farms grew, expeditions were sent into the interior of the country to capture and enslave the indigenous people. These marauders were known as *bandeirantes*, after the flag wielder who ostensibly walked at their head to claim territory. They were mostly made up of culturally disenfranchised offspring of the indigenous Brazilians and the Portuguese – spurned by both communities. São Paulo rose to become the centre of *bandeirante* activity in the 17th century and the *bandeirantes'* expeditions were responsible for the opening up of the country's interior and supplying the indigenous slave trade. A statue by one of Brazil's foremost modernist sculptors, Victor Brecheret, sits on the edge of Ibirapuera in homage to the *bandeirantes*. Yet whilst São Paulo was their headquarters, the *bandeirantes'* success in discovering gold led to the economic demise of the city in the 18th century. The inhabitants rushed to the gold fields in Minas and the *sertão*, leaving São Paulo to fall to ruin and fall under the influence of Rio de Janeiro.

The relative backwardness of the region lasted until the late 19th century when the coffee trade spread west from Rio de Janeiro and Brazil's then richest man – the railway magnate Evangelista de Sousa – established São Paulo as a key city on the newly established railway route to the port of Santos on the coast. Landowners became immensely rich. São Paulo changed from a small town into a financial and residential centre. Exports and imports flowed through Santos via São Paulo and the industrial powerhouse of the country was born. As the city boomed, industries and agriculture fanned outwards to the far reaches of the state.

Between 1885 and the end of the century the boom in coffee and the arrival of large numbers of Europeans transformed the state beyond recognition. By the end of the 1930s more than a million Italians, 500,000 Portuguese, nearly 400,000 Spaniards and 200,000 Japanese had arrived in São Paulo state. São Paulo now has the world's largest Japanese community outside Japan. Their main contribution to the economy has been in horticulture, raising poultry and cotton farming, especially around cities such as Marília. Nowadays, increasing numbers of Japanese-Brazilians work as professionals and in the music industry. Significant numbers of Syrian-Lebanese arrived, too, adding an extra dimension to the cultural diversity of the city. Many of the city's wealthiest dynasties are of Middle Eastern descent. São Paulo also has a large and successful Jewish community. There are two fascinating museums in São Paulo devoted to these immigrants – the Memorial do Imigrante in Mooca (page 45) and the Museu Histórico da Imigração Japonesa in the Japanese dominated neighbourhood of Liberdade.

Much of the immigrant labour that flooded in during the early years of the 20th century was destined for the coffee *fazendas* and farms. Others went to work in the industries that were opening up in the city. By 1941 there were 14,000 factories and by the new millennium metropolitan São Paulo had become the fifth most populous metropolitan area on the planet (according to UN statistics). Today the city covers more than 1500 sq km – three times the size of Paris and, according to the latest information from the Instituto Brasileiro de Geografia e Estatística, greater São Paulo has a population of around 19.96 million, while almost 22% of all Brazilians live in São Paulo state – some 41.6 million people.

Centro Histórico → *For listings, see pages 48-68.*

São Paulo's city centre was once one of the most attractive in South America. English visitors in the 19th century described it as being spacious, green and dominated by terracotta-tiled buildings. There were even macaws and sloths in the trees. Today they are long gone and the centre is dominated by concrete: anonymous edifices, towering over a huddle of interesting churches and cultural centres, and criss-crossed by narrow pedestrian streets. These are lined with stalls selling everything from shoes to electronics, second-hand goods and bric-a-brac. The best way to explore the area is by *metrô* and on foot, but don't stay after dark as the area is insalubrious.

Praça da Sé and around → *Metrô Sé.*
The best place to begin a tour is at the **Praça da Sé**, an expansive square shaded by tropical trees and watched over by the hulking Catholic **Catedral Metropolitana** ① *Praça da Sé, T011-3107 6832, Mon-Sat 0800-1800, Sun 0830-1800, free, Metrô Sé*. This is the heart of the old city and has been the site of Brazil's largest public protests. Crowds gathered here in the late 1980s to demand the end to military rule. And, in 1992, they demanded the impeachment and resignation of the new Republic's second elected president, Fernando Collor – the first in a series of corrupt leaders who, in 1990, had frozen the country's savings accounts and personally pocketed millions. The *praça* is always busy with hawkers, beggars, shoe-shiners and business men rushing between meetings. Evangelists with megaphones proselytize on the steps of the cathedral – a symbol of the war between Christians for the souls of the poor that dominates contemporary urban Brazil. The *praça* is a great spot for street photography though be discreet with your camera and check that you aren't followed after taking your shots. Like São Paulo itself, the cathedral is more remarkable for its size than its beauty and is a somewhat unconvincing mish-mash of neo-Gothic and Renaissance. A narrow nave is squeezed uncomfortably between two monstrous 97-m-high spires beneath a bulbous copper cupola. It was designed in 1912 by the Kassel-born Maximilian Hehl (a professor at the Escola Politécnica da Universidade de São Paulo), inaugurated in the 1950s and fitted with its full complement of 14 towers only in 2002. The interior is bare but for a few stained-glass windows designed in Germany and capitals decorated with Brazilian floral motifs. In the basement there is a vast, pseudo-Gothic crypt. Hehl was also responsible for the Igreja da Consolação (see page 37) and the Catedral de Santos.

Look out for the striking modernist steel sculpture in front of the cathedral in the Praça da Sé, comprising a symmetrical steel plate cut and seemingly folded in the middle along a curvilinear plane. The play of shadow and light around the work – most notable in the early morning or the late afternoon – are hallmarks of its creator, Mineiro graphic artist and sculptor Amílcar de Castro (1920-2002), who revolutionized Brazilian newspaper design in the 1950s before establishing himself at the forefront of the neo-constuctionist movement in Latin America. Together with simple design productive of complex shadow play, his work is characterized by its interaction with the environment. De Castro's sculptures have no protective cover – rust is their paint, and they echo the decaying but modern urban environment of late 20th-century Brazil. De Castro was a key figure in post-War Brazilian art. An obituary in the New York Times described him as "a towering figure in Brazil's art scene" who "gained prominence in the postwar period when Brazilian sculptors, painters and architects were imbued with ambition to break away from the grip of European artistic traditions."

2 São Paulo

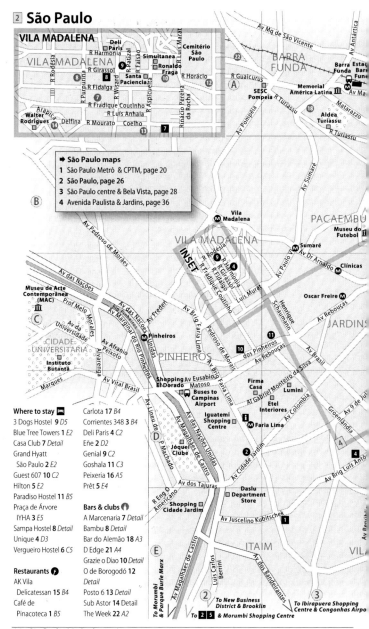

VILA MADALENA

➡ São Paulo maps
1 São Paulo Metrô & CPTM, page 20
2 São Paulo, page 26
3 São Paulo centre & Bela Vista, page 28
4 Avenida Paulista & Jardins, page 36

Where to stay ◻
3 Dogs Hostel **9** *D5*
Blue Tree Towers **1** *E2*
Casa Club **7** *Detail*
Grand Hyatt
São Paulo **2** *E2*
Guest 607 **10** *C2*
Hilton **5** *E2*
Paradiso Hostel **11** *B5*
Praça de Árvore
IYHA **3** *E5*
Sampa Hostel **8** *Detail*
Unique **4** *D3*
Vergueiro Hostel **6** *C5*

Restaurants ⑦
AK Vila
Delicatessan **15** *B4*
Café de
Pinacoteca **1** *B5*

Carlota **17** *B4*
Corrientes 348 **3** *B4*
Deli Paris **4** *C2*
Eñe **2** *D2*
Genial **9** *C2*
Goshala **11** *C3*
Peixeria **16** *A5*
Prêt **5** *E4*

Bars & clubs ◑
A Marcenaria **7** *Detail*
Bambu **8** *Detail*
Bar do Alemão **18** *A3*
D Edge **21** *A4*
Grazie o Diao **10** *Detail*
O de Borogodó **12**
Detail
Posto 6 **13** *Detail*
Sub Astor **14** Detail
The Week **22** *A2*

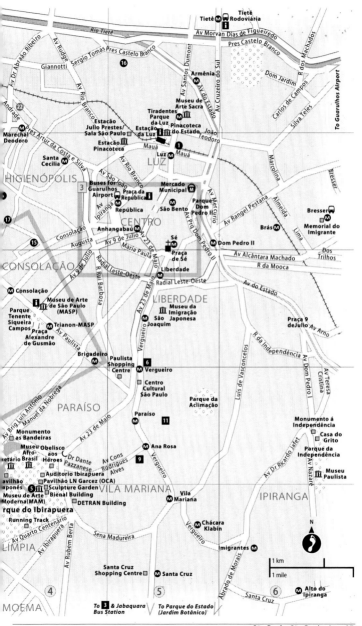

São Paulo São Paulo city ● 27

There are a few other sights of interest around the *praça*. Next door to the cathedral itself and housed in a 1930s art deco building is the **Conjunto Cultural da Caixa** ① *Praça da Sé 111, T011-3321 4400, www.caixacultural.com.br, Tue-Sun 0900-2100, US$2, Metrô Sé*, a gallery that hosts excellent small international art and photography exhibitions by day, and, in the evenings, a boutique theatre. It also has a small banking museum with colonial furniture, on one of its upper floors. Two minutes' walk west of the cathedral, squeezed between ugly modern buildings at the end of Rua Senador Feijó, is the **Igreja da Ordem Terceira de São Francisco** ① *Largo de São Francisco 133, T011-3106 0081, closed at time of publication, Metrô Sé*. This is one of the city's oldest churches, preserving a modest baroque interior (parts of which date to the 17th century) painted in celestial blue. It is quiet and

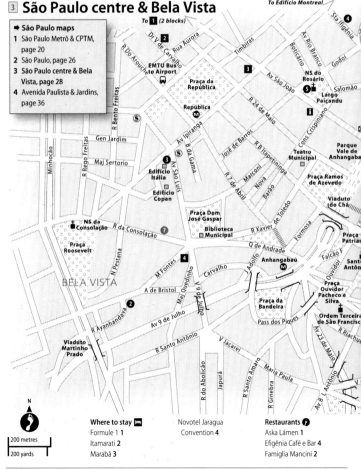

3 São Paulo centre & Bela Vista

➡ São Paulo maps
1 São Paulo Metrô & CPTM, page 20
2 São Paulo, page 26
3 São Paulo centre & Bela Vista, page 28
4 Avenida Paulista & Jardins, page 36

BELA VISTA

N

200 metres
200 yards

Where to stay	Novotel Jaragua	Restaurants
Formule 1 **1**	Convention **4**	Aska Lámen **1**
Itamarati **2**		Efigênia Café e Bar **4**
Marabã **3**		Famiglia Mancini **2**

meditative inside. The exterior is largely an 18th-century excrescence. The church is often referred to as 'O Convento de São Francisco' after a beautiful baroque convent that stood here until the 1930s. This was demolished along with vast swathes of the old colonial centre and sadly the Igreja da Ordem Terceira is in danger of undergoing the same fate – it was condemned in 2008 and remains closed pending donations for a restoration project. There are now only two churches in the centre of one of Brazil's oldest cities that retain any baroque remnants: the Igreja de Santo Antônio (see page 31) and the **Igreja da Ordem Terceira do Carmo** ① *R Rangel Pestana 230, Tue-Sun 0900-2100, free, Metrô Sé*. This church sits just off the far northeastern corner of the Praça da Sé, dates from 1632 and was built by lay brothers, many of whom were former bandeirantes, or their children. It preserves much of its baroque interior, including an impressive ceiling painting, stucco work, religious paintings and artefacts, and an 18th-century gilt baroque altarpiece. It is a peaceful place amidst the hustle and bustle, seldom receiving any visitors.

Pátio do Colégio and around → *Metrô Sé.*
The site of the founding of São Paulo can be reached by walking north from the bottom of the Praça da Sé (furthest from the cathedral) along Rua Santa Teresa and to the Praça Pátio do Colégio. Here lies the **Pátio do Colégio** and **Museu de Anchieta** ① *Praça Pátio do Colégio, T011-3105 6899, www.pateodocollegio.com.br, museum: Tue-Fri 0840-1630, US$1.50, free on the last Sun of the month, Metrô Sé*. Jesuit priests, led by 18-year-old Padre José de Anchieta, arrived here in 1554, when the area was a tiny clearing on a hill in the midst of a vast forest. They made camp and instructed their domicile indigenous Guaraní to construct a simple wattle and daub hut. They inaugurated the building with a celebration of Mass on 25 January 1554, the feast of the conversion of São Paulo. Their simple hut took the saint's name, the 'Colégio de São Paulo de Piratinga'. The hut became a school for converted indigenous Brazilians seduced from the forests around. The school became a church and the church gave its name – São Paulo – to a settlement for *bandeirante* slaving raids into the Brazilian interior. In 1760, the Jesuits were expelled from the city, ironically for opposing the *bandeirantes* – who had established their town around the *colegio* –

and for campaigning in Europe for an end to the indigenous slave trade in Brazil and the Americas, much to the chagrin of the then influential slave and plantation owners in the cities of Salvador, Belém and São Luis. The Pátio do Colégio (as the complex of buildings came to be known) remained, becoming the palace of the fledgling province's Portuguese colonial captains general, and then of its Brazilian imperial governors. The church's tower fell down in 1886 and, shortly after, the whole building was demolished (but for one section of wattle and daub wall). The Jesuits didn't return to São Paulo until 1954 when they immediately set about building an exact replica of their original church and college, which is what stands today.

Most of the buildings are occupied by the **Museu Padre Anchieta**. This preserves, amongst other items, a modernist (and not altogether sympathetic painting) of the priest, by Italian Albino Menghini, bits of his corpse (which is now that of a saint after Anchieta was canonized by Pope John Paul II), a 17th-century font used to baptize the indigenous Brazilians and a collection of Guaraní art and artefacts from the colonial era. The Pátio has a great little al fresco café with a view, serving good snacks and light meals. The clergy in the college have long maintained an interest in a 'preferential option for the poor' which, since the suppression of Liberation Theology in Brazil, has been out of fashion. Members of the college joyously celebrated the election of the new Jesuit pope, Francisco, in 2013. After a parade for the poor children of the city's periphery, dozens of children dressed as St Francis climbed on the stage singing the prayer of St Francis with a poster showing the pope's face with the words "Papa Francisco, O Papa dos pobres" written beneath.

The exhibition spaces, cultural centres and concert halls of the **Centro Cultural Banco do Brasil** ① *R Álvares Penteado 112, T011-3113 3651, www.bb.com.br, Mon-Fri 0900-1800, free except for exhibitions, Metrô Sé or São Bento*, can be reached by turning immediately west from the front of the Pátio do Colégio along Rua do Tesouro and then right for a block along Rua Álvares Penteado. These are housed in an attractive art nouveau building with a pretty glass ceiling. Many of the galleries are contained within the banks original vaults, some of which retain their massive iron doors. The cultural centre has a diverse programme of art and photography shows, cultural events and, in the evenings, theatre, music and cinema. It is always worth a visit.

Mosteiro do São Bento and around → *Metrô São Bento.*

The most beautiful of all the churches in São Paulo is the Benedictine Basilica de Nossa Senhora de Assunção, known as the **Mosteiro de São Bento** ① *Largo São Bento, T011-3228 3633, www.mosteiro.org.br, Mon-Fri 0600-1800, Sat and Sun 0600-1200 and 1600-1800, Latin Mass with Gregorian chant Sun 1000; Latin vespers Mon-Fri 1725, Sat 1700, free, Metrô São Bento.* Benedictines arrived on this site in 1598, shortly after the Jesuits and, like them, proceeded to proselytize the indigenous people. Despite their long history in the city the monastery is a modern church dating from 1914. It was designed by Munich-based architect Richard Bernl in homage to the English Norman style. Its façade is strikingly similar to Southwell cathedral in Nottinghamshire, though with added Rhineland roofs and baroque revival flourishes. However, few visit São Bento for the exterior. The church preserves a striking Beuronese interior painted by Dom Adelbert Gresnicht, a Dutch Benedictine monk who died in 1956. The style is named after techniques developed by Benedictines in the monastery of Beuron in southwest Germany in the late 19th and early 20th centuries. It finds much inspiration in Byzantine art and is characterized by compressed perspective and iconic, almost exaggerated colours. São Bento is one of the finest Beuronese churches in the world. The stained glass (and much of the statuary) is also by Dom Adelbert. Most of the windows show scenes from the life of St Benedict with the most beautiful, at the far end of the nave, showing Our Lady ascending to heaven guided by the Holy Spirit in the form of a dove. The church has Brazil's finest organ which is given its own festival in November and December every year. This being a Benedictine monastery, there is of course a shop, which sells delicious sweets made by the monks in their bakery. Just across from the monastery on the Largo São Bento and next to the *metrô* there's a peaceful, surprisingly green little café, the **Efigênia Café and Bar** (see page 51). It's a good spot for a coffee.

Immediately in front of the monastery, at the corner of Avenida São João and Rua Libero Badaró, is the **Edifício Martinelli (Martinelli Building)** ① *Av São João 35, not open to the public, Metrô São Bento*. This was the city's first skyscraper and, when it was built, looked out over a sea of terracotta roofs and handsome tree-lined avenues. The building pays homage to New York's upper east side but while colonial São Paulo was unique and beautiful, the buildings that replaced it are less original or distinguished than the New York edifices they longed to imitate. A block south, next to the Viaduto do Chá at the bottom of Rua Dr Falcão Filho, is another early São Paulo skyscraper, the bulky **Edifício Francisco Matarazzo** ① *Dr Falcão Filho,56, Centro, T011-3248 1135, Mon-Fri 1000-1700*, built in 1937 and known locally as 'Banespinha'. The building is now occupied by the mayoral office. While it's not officially open to the public, try and visit if you can to see one of Latin America's finest and largest skyscraper gardens (on the 14th floor), which boasts more than 300 species of flowering plants and towering trees, the largest of which are over 20 m tall. There are terrific views from the perimetral veranda.

A few blocks northeast and just round the corner from the monastery is Banespinha's big brother – the **Banespa** building, officially known as the **Edifício Altino Arantes** or **Santander Cultural** ① *R João Bricola 24 (Metrô São Bento), T011-3249 7466, Mon-Fri 1000-1500, free, ID is required, visits limited to 10 mins (dusk visits are limited to those with prior appointments), daypacks must be left in reception, no tripods or bags can be taken to the viewing deck*. It's a homage to New York, looking a bit like a wan Empire State Building, small enough to collapse under the weight of King Kong. The view of the city from the observatory is awe-inspiring. A sea of concrete spires stretches to the city limits on every horizon, fringed with vast *favelas* and new distant neighbourhoods and with hundreds of helicopters whirling overhead like giant buzzing flies.

Less than 50 m from the Edifício Altino Arantes is the oldest church in São Paulo's city centre, the **Igreja de Santo Antônio** ① *Praça do Patriarca s/n, Mon-Fri 0900-1600, free, Metrô São Bento*, with parts dating from 1592. It was fully restored in 2005 and together with the Igreja do Carmo is the only church in the city centre with a baroque interior – although much of what you see today is from reforms in 1899. It's another tranquil spot in the middle of one of the world's busiest city centres.

The streets between São Bento and Luz offer some of the best people-watching and shopping adventures in the city. The partially covered **Rua 25 de Março** ① *daily 0700-1800, Metrô São Bento shopping complex*, runs north to Rua Paula Sousa and Metrô Luz station and is one of the best places in Brazil to buy quality clothing and electronics at a low price. Two blocks east of 25 de Marco along Rua Comendador Afonso Kherlakian is the beautiful art deco **Mercado Municipal** ① *R da Cantareira 306, Centro, T011-3326 3401, www.mercadomunicipal.com.br, Mon-Sat 0600-1800, Sun 0600-1600, free, Metrô São Bento or Luz; see Shopping, page 64*. It's an easy walk from the market or Rua 25 de Março to Luz, though caution should be observed at all times. The streets to the west, between the centre and Júlio Prestes station, should be avoided especially after dark. This is a notorious area for crack dealing.

Praça da República → *Metrô República.*

This tree-lined square a few blocks northwest of the Viaduto do Chá was the centre of the city's Vanity Fair – the place to see and be seen – in the late 19th century. It was then known as the Largo dos Curros, but was re-branded for the Republic after the overthrow of the monarchy. Wealthy Paulistanos would gather here to watch rodeios and touradas. Like the Praça da Sé it has long been an important centre of public protest. On 23 May 1932, towards the end of the Constitutional Revolution, thousands gathered here in front of the old Partido Popular Paulista to protest against the Vargas regime. Many were shot dead as a result. There is a lively arts and crafts market in the square every Saturday and Sunday 0900-1700.

A few interesting buildings and sights lie nearby. These include the **Edifício and Terraço Itália** ① *Av Ipiranga 344, T011-2189 2990 and T011-2189 2929, www.edificioitalia. com.br, restaurant: www.terracoitalia.com.br, US$5, Metrô República,* a rather unremarkable restaurant in the city's tallest building with a truly remarkable view from the observation deck. Photographers should aim to arrive half an hour before sunset for the best balance of natural and artificial light, and bring a tripod, though you should be prepared for the officials to try and charge you extra for its usage. The skyscraper immediately in front of the *terraço* is Oscar Niemeyer's **Edifício Copan** ① *Av Ipiranga 200, not open to the public though some visitors are allowed to go to the terraço at the discretion of security, Metrô República,* built in 1951 in a spate of design by the architect, which included the nearby **Edifício Montreal** ① *Av Ipiranga at Cásper Líbero,* and the **Edifício Califórnia** ① *R Barão de Itapetininga.* Edifício Copan is the setting for *Arca sem Noé – histórias do edifício Copan,* a series of memorable short stories, dissecting daily life and class in São Paulo written by the Paulistano writer Regina Rheda (published in English as *First World, Third Class and Other Tales of the Global Mix* in 2005). A crypt-like art space, the **Pivô** ① *Av Ipiranga 200, lj 48, T011-3255 8703,* opened in 2013 in the building's basement, showing contemporary art with past shows including US sculptor David Adamo.

From the corner of Praça da República, a 10-minute walk southeast along Rua 24 de Maio brings you back into the main part of the city centre and Metrô Anhangabaú, via the **Teatro Municipal Opera House** ① *Praça Ramos de Azevedo s/n, T011-3397 0300, www. prefeitura.sp.gov.br/cidade/secretarias/cultura/theatromunicipal, box office Mon-Fri 1000-1900, Sat 1000-1700, tickets from US$5, Metrô Anhangabaú, República or São Bento.* Based on the 1874 beaux-arts Palais Garnier but stunted in comparison, it is made of dull stone with huge baroque flourishes on the roof which make it look inelegantly top heavy. It is altogether more impressive within, with its stained glass, opulent hallways and public areas together with its stage and auditorium undergoing thorough renovation and modernization in late 2011. Maria Callas, Nureyev and Fonteyn and Duke Ellington have all graced the concert hall and it is now once again one of Brazil's finest venues for classical music and dance and the home to a body of performers which include the Orquestra Sinfônica Municipal, Orquestra Experimental de Repertório, Balé da Cidade de São Paulo, Quarteto de Cordas da Cidade de São Paulo, Coral Lírico, Coral Paulistano and the Escolas de Dança e de Música de São Paulo.

Next to the theatre is the **Viaduto do Chá,** a steel bridge riding over the attractive but scruffy Vale de Anhangabaú park and the traffic-heavy Avenida 23 de Maio and 9 de Julho urban highways.

North of the centre → *For listings, see pages 48-68.*

Luz → *Metrô Luz or Metrô Tiradentes, Metrô/CPTM Luz or Júlio Prestes.*

Some of São Paulo's finest museums are to be found a few kilometres north of the city centre in the neighbourhood of Luz. The area is dominated by two striking 19th- and early 20th-century railway stations, both in use today: the **Estação da Luz** ① *Praça da Luz 1, T0800-550121 for information on suburban trains*, and **Estação Júlio Prestes** ① *Praça Júlio Prestes 51, www.estacoesferroviarias.com.br/j/jprestes.htm*. The former marked the realization of a dream for O Ireneu Evangelista de Sousa, the Visconde de Mauá, who was Brazil's first industrial magnate. A visit to London in the 1840s convinced de Sousa that Brazil's future lay in rapid industrialization – a path he followed with the founding of an ironworks employing some 300 workers from England and Scotland. It made him a millionaire and in 1854 he opened his first railway, designed and run by the British. It linked Jundiaí, in the heart of the São Paulo coffee region, with Santos on the coast via what was then the relatively small city of São Paulo. The line is still extant; though passenger trains only run on the Jundiaí to São Paulo section (see Linha 7 Rubi, page 66). The grandness of the Estação de Luz station, which was completed in 1900, attests to the fact that the city quickly grew wealthy by exploiting its position at the railway junction. By the time the Estação Júlio Prestes was built, Britannia no longer ruled the railways. This next station was modelled on Grand Central and Penn in New York. In 1999 the enormous 1000-sq-m grand hall was converted into the magnificent 1500-seat cathedral-like **Sala São Paulo Concert Hall** ① *Praça Júlio Prestes 51, T011-3337 9573, www.salasaopaulo.art.br, guided visits Mon-Fri 1300-1630, Sat 1330, Sun 1400 (when there is an evening performance) or 1230 (when there is an afternoon performance), US$2.50, free on Sun, foreigners should book ahead through the website as English-speaking guides must be arranged, box office T011-3223 3966, Mon-Fri 1000-1800, Sat 1000-1630, concerts from US$10, Metrô/CPTM Luz or Júlio Prestes*, Brazil's most prestigious classical music venue (see page 60) and home to the **Orquestra Sinfônica do Estado de São Paulo** ① *www.osesp.art.br*, and choir, one of the best in South America, conducted by Marin Alsop, who is also the music director of the Baltimore Symphony Orchestra.

The city's finest collection of Brazilian art lies 100 m from the Estação da Luz in the **Pinacoteca do Estado** ① *Praça da Luz 2, T011-3324 0933, www.pinacoteca.org.br, Tue-Wed 1000-1730 (last entry at 1700), Thu 1000-2200, Fri-Sun 1000-1730 (last entry at 1730), US$3, free on Sat, Metrô/CPTM Luz, excellent museum shop and café*. Here you will find works by Brazilian artists from the colonial and imperial eras, together with paintings by the founders of Brazilian Modernism, such as Lasar Segall, Tarsila do Amaral, Candido Portinari and Alfredo Volpi. The gallery also contains sculpture by Rodin, Victor Brecheret and contemporary works by artists such as the Nipo-Brazilian painter Tomie Ohtake. The excellent photography gallery in the basement displays some of the world's greatest black-and-white photographers, many of whom are from Brazil. The museum overlooks the **Parque da Luz** ① *Praça da Luz s/n, Tue-Sun, 1000-1800, free*, a lovely shady fenced-in green space dotted with modernist sculpture and shaded by large tropical figs and palms. This was the city's first park, opening in 1825. It was fully refurbished (down to the lovely wrought iron faux-French bandstand) in the new millennium. Take care in this area after dark.

The Pinacoteca's sister gallery, the **Estação Pinacoteca and Memorial da Resistência Museum** ① *Largo General Osório 66, T011-3335 4990, www.pinacoteca.org.br, www. memorialdaresistenciasp.org.br, Tue-Sun 1000-1730, US$3, free for the Memorial da Resistência and for the galleries on Sat, very good café-restaurant, Metrô/CPTM Luz and Júlio Prestes*, is just over 500 m west of the Pinacoteca along Rua Mauá, next to the Estação Júlio Prestes and Sala São. The *estação* preserves 200 of the country's finest modernist paintings from the archive of the Fundação José e Paulina Nemirovsky, including further key pieces by Tarsila do Amaral, Emiliano Di Cavalcanti, Portinari Anita Malfatti, Victor Brecheret and Lasar Segall. International art includes Chagall, Picasso and Braque. The building was once the headquarters of the Departamento Estadual de Ordem Politica e Social do Estado de São Paulo (DEOPS/SP) – the counter-insurgency wing of the Policia Militar police force. Thousands of Paulistanos were tortured and killed here between 1940 and 1983, during the Vargas years and the military dictatorship. The Memorial da Resistência de São Paulo Museum on the ground floor tells their story in grisly detail – through panels, documents and photographs – and shows how the CIA supported the oppression.

Across the Praça da Luz to the south of the Pinacoteca and housed in the Estação da Luz railway station is the **Museu da Língua Portuguesa** ① *Praça da Luz, T011-3322 0080, www.museulinguaportuguesa.org.br, Tue 1000-2200, Wed-Sun 1000-1800 (last visit 1700), US$3, free Sat, Metrô/CPTM Luz*. This excellent little museum has captivating interactive and audio-visual exhibits in tastefully laid-out galleries devoted to everything Portuguese – from high literary art (with excerpts from seminal works) to street slang, song and correct grammar.

Diagonally across busy Avenida Tiradentes from the Pinacotaca and some 400 m to the north, is the **Museu de Arte Sacra** ① *Av Tiradentes 676, T011-3227 7687, www. museuartesacra.org.br, Tue-Sun 1000-1800, US$3, Metrô Tiradentes, Metrô/CPTM Luz*. This superb little museum is often overlooked by visitors, yet it is one of the finest of its kind in the Americas. The collection is housed in a large wing of one of the city's most distinguished colonial buildings, the early 19th-century Mosteiro da Luz. Parts of the monastery are still home to Conceptionist sisters and the entire complex is imbued with a restful sense of serenity. Even those who are not interested in church art will find the galleries a delightfully peaceful haven from the frenetic chaos of São Paulo. The collection, however, is priceless and of international importance. Rooms house objects and artefacts from lavish monstrances and ecclesiastical jewellery to church altarpieces. Of particular note is the statuary, with pieces by many of the most important Brazilian baroque masters. Amongst objects by Portuguese sculptor and ceramicist Frei Agostinho da Piedade (1580-1661), his Brazilian student, Frei Agostinho de Jesus (c 1600-1661), Mineiro master painter Manuel da Costa (Mestre) Athayde (1762-1830), and Mestre Valentim (c 1745-1813), is a wonderful Mary Magdalene by Francisco Xavier de Brito, displaying an effortless unity of motion and melancholy contemplation. There are sculptures by (anonymous) Brazilian indigenous artists, a majestic African-Brazilian São Bento (with blue eyes) and an extraordinarily detailed 18th-century Neapolitan nativity crib comprising almost 2000 pieces, which is the most important of its kind outside Naples.

Barra Funda and Higienópolis → *Metrô Palmeiras-Barra Funda, CPTM Barra Funda.*
The Cyclopean group of modernist concrete buildings making up the **Memorial da América Latina** ① *Av Mário de Andrade 664, next to Metrô Barra Funda, T011-3823 4600, www.memorial.org.br, Tue-Fri 0900-2100, Sat 0900-1800, Sun 1000-1800, free*, were designed by Oscar Niemeyer and built in March 1989. They comprise a monumental

85,000-sq-m-complex of curvi-linear galleries, conference spaces, walkways, bridges and squares, broken by an ugly, urban highway and dotted with imposing sculptures. The largest of these is in the shape of an outstretched hand. The complex was built with the grand aim of integrating Latin American nations, culturally and politically, but it is sorely underused. Occasional shows include the annual Latin American art exhibition in the Pavilhão de Criatividade.

A few kilometres west of Barra Funda – a quick hop along the CPTM's Linha Rubi – in the emerging nightlife district of **Água Branca**, is **SESC Pompeia** ① *R Clélia 93, T011-3871 7700, www.sescsp.org.br, CPTM Água Branca, 10 mins' walk southeast or US$3 in a taxi*, an arts complex housed in a striking post-industrial building designed by the Italian-Brazilian Le Corbusier-influenced architect Lina Bo Bardi (who was also responsible for MASP, see below). Together with SESC Vila Mariana (see page 41), SESC showcases some of the best medium-sized musical acts in the city, hosting names such as João Bosco, CéU and Otto. It is a vibrant place, with a theatre, exhibitions, workshops, restaurant and café, as well as a gym and areas for sunbathing and watching television.

The upper middle-class neighbourhood of **Higienópolis** lies between Barra Funda and Consolação. It is a favourite haunt of artists and musicians a number of whom live in the **Bretagne building** ① *Av Higienópolis 938, T011-3667 2516*, one of a handful of delightful mid-20th-century blocks of flats. With curved lines, brilliant mosaics and polished stone it looks like a film set for an arty 1960s film. Higienópolis also boasts one of the city's plushest shopping malls, the **Patio Higienópolis** ① *Av Higienópolis 618, T011-3823 2300, www. patiohigienopolis.com.br*.

West of the centre → *For listings, see pages 48-68.*

Avenida Paulista → *Metrô Vergueiro or Paraíso for the southeastern end of Paulista.*
Southwest of the Centro Histórico, Avenida Paulista is lined by skyscrapers and thick with traffic six lanes wide. It is one of São Paulo's classic postcard shots and locals like to compare it to Fifth Avenue in New York. In truth, it's more commercial and lined with functional buildings, most of which are unremarkable individually but awe-inspiring as a whole.

The avenue was founded in 1891 by the Uruguayan engineer Joaquim Eugênio de Lima, who wanted to build a Paulistano Champs-Élysées. After he built a mansion on Avenida Paulista, many coffee barons followed suit and by the 1930s, Avenida Paulista had become the city's most fashionable promenade. The mansions and rows of stately trees that sat in front of them were almost all demolished in the 1950s to make way for decidedly less beautiful office buildings; these were in turn demolished in the 1980s as banks and multinationals established their headquarters here. A handful of mansions however remain, including the **Casa das Rosas** ① *Av Paulista 37, T011-3285 6986, www. poiesis.org.br/casadasrosas, Tue-Sat 1000-2200, Sun 1000-1800, free*, one of the last of the mansions to have been built and now a literary centre devoted principally preserving the 35,000-volume library of the poet Haroldo de Campos, which includes a number of rare, autographed first editions by writers such as Otavio Paz and João Cabral de Melo Neto.

The highlight of Avenida Paulista is the **Museu de Arte de São Paulo** (**MASP**) ① *Av Paulista 1578, T011-3251 5644, www.masp.art.br, Tue-Wed and Fri-Sun 1000-1800, Thu 1000-2000, US$7.50, Metrô Trianon-MASP*. This is the most important gallery in the southern hemisphere, preserving some of Europe's greatest paintings. If it were in the US or Europe it would be as busy as the Prado or the Guggenheim, but here, aside from the occasional noisy group of schoolchildren, the gallery is invariably deserted. Even at weekends, visitors can stop and stare at a Rembrandt or a Velazquez at their leisure. The museum has a far larger collection than it is able to display and only a tiny fraction reaches the walls of the modest-sized international gallery and as the collection is frequently rotated it's hard to predict what will be on show at any one time. France gets star-billing, with 11 Renoirs, 70 Degas, and a stream of works by Monet, Manet, Cezanne, Toulouse-Lautrec and Gauguin. Renaissance Italy is represented by a Raphael Resurrection, an impeccable Bellini and a series of exquisite late 15th-century icons. The remaining walls are adorned with paintings by Bosch, Goya, Van Dyck, Turner, Constable and many others, cherry-picked from post-War Europe. A gallery downstairs, the **Galeria Clemente de Faria**, houses temporary exhibitions, mostly by contemporary Brazilian artists and photographers, and the museum has a decent and good-value restaurant serving buffet lunches (see page 52) and a small but tasteful gift shop. On Sunday, an antiques fair is held in the open space beneath the museum.

There are two more galleries/art centres on Avenida Paulista. **Itaú Cultural** ⓘ *Av Paulista149, T011-2168 1777, Tue-Fri 0900-2000, Sat and Sun 1100-2000, free*, which principally showcases contemporary art, theatre and quality music, and which has a small

4 Avenida Paulista & Jardins

numismatic museum that was renovated in 2013. **FIESP** ① *Av Paulista1313, T011-3146 7405, Mon 1100-1930, Tue-Sat 1000-1930, Sun 1000-1830, free,* has free Sunday concerts at midday and a regular theatre programme, including performances for children.

Opposite MASP is the **Parque Tenente Siqueira Campos** ① *R Peixoto Gomide 949 and Av Paulista, daily 0700-1830,* also known as Parque Trianon, covering two blocks on either side of Alameda Santos. It is a welcome, luxuriant, green area located in what is now the busiest part of the city. The vegetation includes native plants typical of the Mata Atlântica. Next to the park is the smaller Praça Alexandre de Gusmão.

Consolação and the Pacaembu Museu do Futebol → *Metrô Consolação.*

Consolação, which lies between the northeastern end of Avenida Paulista and the Edifício Italia and Praça República in the city centre, is emerging as the edgiest and most exciting nocturnal neighbourhood in São Paulo. Until a few years it was home to little more than rats, sleazy strip bars, street-walkers and curb-crawlers, but now it harbours a thriving alternative weekend scene. Its untidy streets are lined with graffiti-scrawled shop fronts, the deep velvet-red of open bar doors, go-go clubs with heavy-set bouncers outside, and makeshift street bars. On Friday and Saturday nights hundreds of young Paulistanos downn bottles of cooler-fresh Bohemia beer at rickety metal tables, and lines of sharply dressed and well-toned 20- and 30-somethings queue to enter a gamut of fashionable bars, clubs and pounding gay venues, including one of Brazil's most exciting underground venues, **Studio SP** (see Bars and clubs, page 57).

Just north of Consolação, on the other side of the Sacramento Cemetery and rushing Avenida Doutour Arnaldo, is the beautiful art deco football stadium **Estádio Pacaembu**, which hosts domestic games and big international rock concerts. It sits in a square named after Charles Miller, the Englishman who brought football to Brazil. Inside is the **Museu do Futebol** ① *Metrô Clinicas, Estádio do Pacaembu, Praça Charles Miller, T011-3664 3848, www.museudofutebol.org.br, Tue-Sun 0900-1700, US$3, free on Thu, children under 7 free, restaurants next to the museum in the stadium, Metrô Sumaré (20-min walk),* which cost US$15 million and which was inaugurated by Pelé in September 2008.

500 metres (approx)
500 yards (approx)

The 2014 FIFA World Cup™, which Brazil has won more often than any other team, is the principal focus. One gallery is devoted to the tournament, profiling the games and what was happening in the world at the time, and telling both stories through video footage, photographs, memorabilia and newspaper cuttings. Music from the likes of Ary Barroso and Jorge Ben forms the soundtrack, along with recordings of cheering fans. A second gallery showcases Brazil's greatest stars, including Garrincha, Falcão, Zico, Bebeto, Didi, Romário, Ronaldo, Gilmar, Gérson, Sócrates, Rivelino, Ronaldo (who is known as Ronaldinho or Ronaldinho Fenomeno in Brazil) and, of course, Pelé. The shirt he wore during the 1970 World Cup™ final – a game frequently cited as the greatest ever played when Brazil beat Italy 4-1 to take the title for the third time – receives pride of place. A third gallery is more interactive, offering visitors the chance to dribble and shoot at goals and test their knowledge on football facts and figures. If coming by *metrô* look out for the 44 striking panels showing local people with poems and letters super-imposed on their faces, by Paulistano artist and German resident Alex Fleming. They're situated in the gallery running over Aveninda Sumaré

Jardins → *Metrô Consolação or Oscar Freire (Linha Amarela from 2012).*
Immediately west of Avenida Paulista, an easy 10-minute walk from Metrô Consolação along Rua Haddock Lobo, is the plush neighbourhood of Jardins. This is by far the most pleasant area to stay in São Paulo; it has the best restaurants, shops, cafés and tranquil spots for people-watching, or an urban boutique browse. Jardins is, in reality, a series of neighbourhoods – each with its own name. The stretches closest to Paulista are known as **Cerqueira César** (to the northwest) and **Jardim Paulista** (to the southeast). These two areas have the bulk of the boutique shops, swanky hotels and chic restaurants. The most self-consciously chic of all is the cross section between Rua Oscar Freire, Rua Bela Cintra and Rua Haddock Lobo, where even the poodles wear collars with designer labels and everyone, from the shop owner to the doorman, addresses each other as '*Querida*' (Darling).

Immediately west of Jardim Paulista and Cerqueira César, and separated from those neighbourhoods by a stately city highway preserving a handful of coffee Baron mansions (Avenida Brasil), are three more jardins. **Jardim Paulistano** is dominated by Avenida Gabriel Monteiro da Silva, which is lined by very expensive, internationally renowned home decor and furniture stores. Between Jardim Paulistano and Ibirapuera Park are **Jardim America** and **Jardim Europa**, both made up of leafy streets lined with vast mansion houses, almost completely hidden behind towering walls topped with razor wire and formidable electric fencing. Their idyllic seclusion is spoilt only by the stench of raw *favela* sewage from the nearby Rio Pinheiros.

The **Museu Brasileiro da Escultura (MUBE)** ① *Av Europa 218, T011-2594 2601, www. mube.art.br, Tue-Sun 1000-1900, free,* from Metrô Consolação, corner of R Augusta and Av, take bus 702P-42, marked 'Butantã', showcases contemporary Brazilian sculpture through visiting exhibitions. Most are rather lacklustre and the museum merits a visit more for the building itself, which is by Brazil's Prtizker prize-winning architect Paulo Mendes da Rocha. Like many Brazilian architects Espírito Santo-born Rocha is celebrated for his inventive, minimalist use of concrete. The museum is made up of a series of massive, grey, bunker-like concrete blocks which contrast starkly with the surrounding gardens (by Burle Marx), but which integrate them with the underground exhibition spaces.

The **Museu da Casa Brasileira** ① *Av Brigadeiro Faria Lima 2705, T011-3032 3727, www. mcb.sp.gov.br, Tue-Sun 1000-1800, US$2, Sun free; from CPTM Cidade Jardim it's a 10-min walk: from Pinheiros head east along R Professor Artur Ramos to Av Brigadeiro Faria Lima,* devoted to design, architecture and decoration and housed in a stately 1940s mansion, preserves a collection of antique (mostly baroque) Brazilian and Portuguese and contemporary international furniture and examples of iconic Brazilian design. The museum also hosts the annual Prêmio Design MCB design awards, which has become one of the most celebrated in Brazil. Temporary exhibition spaces showcase the winners and the museum has a pleasant garden (with live music on Sundays) and a good café-restaurant.

The **Museu da Imagem de Do Som (MIS)** ⓘ *Av Europa, 158, Jardim Europa, T011-2117 4777, www.mis-sp.org.br, Tue-Fri 1200-2200, Sat and Sun 1100-2100, free, exhibitions from US$3,* has exciting temporary exhibitions (in 2013 these included the first Latin American show by the dissident Chines artist and photographer Ai Weiwei), an arts cinema, sound labs, a huge audio and visual archive and weekly club nights with DJs or live music. **Chez MIS** in the museum is one of the city's best new restaurants.

A number of Brazil's most prestigious commercial art galleries lie within Jardins. The prestigious **Galeria Luisa Strina** ⓘ *R Padre João Manuel 755, Jardim Paulista, T011-3088 2471, www.galerialuisastrina.com.br,* represents and shows leading contemporary artists such as Olafur Eliasson, Cildo Meirelles, Leonor Antunes, Pedro Motta and Erick Beltrán. **Dan Galeria** ⓘ *R Estados Unidos 1638, Jardim América, T011-3082 4223, www.dangaleria. com.br,* sells works by some of the most important contemporary and deceased Brazilian including Benedito Calixto, Amelia Toledo, Anita Malfatti, Cícero Dias, Tarsila do Amaral, Volpi, Tomie Ohtake, Candido Portinari and Lygia Clark. The **Galeria Nara Roesler** ⓘ *Av Europa 655, Jardim Europa, T011-3063 2344, www.nararoesler.com.br,* deals with contemporary art since 1975, representing artists including Abraham Palatnik, Antonio Dias, Hélio Oiticica and Milton Machado. **Amoa Konoya** ⓘ *R João Moura 1002, Jardim América, T011-3061 0639, www.amoakonoya.com.br, Mon-Sat 0900-1800,* is devoted to art from Brazil's traibal peoples.

Vila Madalena and Pinheiros → *Metrô Madalena, Fradique Coutinho (under construction).*
If Jardins is São Paulo's upper East Side or Bond Street, Vila Madalena and neighbouring Pinheiros are its East Village or Notting Hill – still fashionable, but younger, less ostentatiously moneyed and with more of a skip in their step. Streets are crammed with bars, restaurants and an array of the city's freshest designer labels, clambering over the steep hills and buzzing with young and arty middle class Paulistanos. Younger boutique brands have set up shop in Vila Madalena (see Shopping, page 60). Galleries such as **Choque Cultural** ⓘ *R Medeiros de Albuquerque 250, Vila Madalena, T011-3061 2365, Mon-Fri 1000-1700, Sat 1100-1700, www.choquecultural.com.br,* sell work by the newest wave of the city's increasingly famous street artists (as well as prints available online) and the Beco do Batman (Rua Gonçalo Afonso) – an alley daubed with the latest brightly coloured art from the city's streets – has become a must-see both for impoverished graffiti artists and well-to-do gallery browsers.

With music on every corner in both neighbourhoods – from spit-and-sawdust samba bars to mock-Bahian *forró* clubs and well-established live music venues – the neighbourhoods attract rich and famous boho residents. Seu Jorge lives and drinks in Vila Madalena, as does leading avant garde musician, Max de Castro. There are a few art galleries worth a browse. They include the **Instituto Tomie Ohtake** ⓘ *R dos Coropés 88, T011-3814 0705, www.institutotomieohtake.org.br, Tue-Fri 1000-1800, US$1.50,* a monolithic, rather ungainly red and purple tower by Unique Hotel architect Ruy Ohtake. It has galleries inside devoted to the work of his Japanese-Brazilian artist mother, Tomie, and a series of other exhibition halls with work by up-and-coming artists. To get there, go to Metrô Vila Madalena, then take bus 701-10 southwest along Rua Purpurina and Rua Fradique Coutinho, getting off at the stop at Fradique Coutinho 1331. Leave the stop and turn right onto Rua Wisard. After 200 m continue onto Rua dos Miranhas. After 400 m continue onto Rua dos Tamanás and after 150 m turn right into Rua dos Coropés.

As well as **Choque Cultural** (see above), commercial galleries in the area include: **Recorte Transversal** ① *R Fidalga 545, Vila Madalena, T011-3392 5287, www.galeriatransversal.com.br, Tue-Thu 1000-2000, Fri 1000-1900, Sat 1000-1800, by appointment,* with a sister gallery in Barra Funda opened in 2013, devoted principally to Brazilian contemporary art; and **Fortes Vilaça** ① *R Fradique Coutinho 1500, Vila Madalena, and R James Holland 71, Barra Funda, T011-3032 7066,* leading Brazilian contemporary artists including Os Gêmeos, Ernesto Neto and Nuno Ramos as well as a handful of international (mostly British) names such as Cerith Wyn Evans.

On Sundays there's an open-air market in the Praça Benedito Calixto (www. pracabeneditocalixto.com.br) in Pinheiros selling antiques, curios, clothing and general bric-a-brac. It's a very hippy chic, attracting the city's middle and upper-middle classes, many of whom gather to dance samba or listen to live *chorinho* (from 1430). There are dozens of cafés, snack bars on and around the praça, as well as simple restaurants serving feijoada, escondidinho and other hearty fare.

South of the centre → *For listings, see pages 48-68.*

Liberdade → *Metrô Liberdade.*

Liberdade was the first centre for the Japanese community in São Paulo, a city with more ethnic Japanese than any other outside Japan. It lies directly south of the Praça da Sé and can easily be reached from there on foot in under 10 minutes. There are all manner of Asian shops selling everything from woks to *manga* and the streets are illuminated by lights designed to resemble Japanese lanterns. A market selling Asian produce and food is held every Sunday in the Praça da Liberdade and there are many excellent Japanese restaurants.

The **Museu da Imigração Japonesa** ① *R São Joaquim 381, 3rd floor, T011-3209 5465, www.nihonsite.com/muse, Tue-Sun 1330-1730, US$3, Metrô Liberdade,* in the Japanese-Brazilian cultural centre, is a modern, well-kept little museum with exhibitions telling the story of the Japanese migration to Brazil, with a replica of the first ship that brought the Japanese to Brazil, reconstructions of early Japanese Brazilian houses, artefacts and clothing.

Bela Vista

Bela Vista lies immediately west of Liberdade and east of Consolação between the city centre and Avenida Paulista. In the late 19th and early 20th century the neighbourhood was a centre of Italian immigration. It is a higgledy-piggledy mass of small streets lined with residential houses. There are few sights of interest but the area is a pleasant place for a wander, especially at weekends. On Sunday there is an antiques market, the **Feira das Antiguidades** ① *Praça Dom Orione, Bixiga, Bela Vista, Sun 1000-1500, sometimes with live chorinho.* There are Italianate houses nearby on Rua dos Ingleses, and a number of little cafés and bars. During carnival the **Vai Vai Samba School** ① *R São Vicente 276, T011-3266 2581, www.vaivai.com.br, US$7.50 for the carnival party,* opens its doors to as many as 4000 visitors who come to dance samba and parade through the nearby streets. They often throw a smaller *feijoada* party at weekends. **Rua Avanhandava**, which runs off Rua Martins Fontes in the north of Bela Vista, was closed to traffic in 2007, and has since become one of the prettiest streets in the neighbourhood, lined with traditional Italian restaurants.

Oscar Niemeyer in São Paulo

São Paulo is home to many impressive buildings by South America's most important modernist architect, the late Oscar Niemeyer. Many have only opened to the public in the last few years.

→ **Auditório Ibirapuera** (Parque Ibirapuera), a stunning door-wedge shape with a sinuous portal entrance.

→ **Bienal buildings** (Parque Ibirapuera), home of Fashion Week and the Art Bienal; the serpentine walkways are fabulous.

→ **Edifício Copan** (Centro/Consolação), a tower built as a swirling wave.

→ **Ibirapuera museums and walkways** (Parque Ibirapuera), minimalist blocks with vast interior spaces linked by classic Niemeyer curving walkways.

→ **Memorial da América Latina** (Barra Funda), a gargantuan concrete wave between towering rectilinear monoliths.

→ **The Oca** (Parque Ibirapuera), a bright white concrete half-dome, in homage to indigenous communal houses.

→ **Sambódromo do Anhembi** (Anhembi), the stadium venue for São Paulo carnival built right after Rio's.

Paraíso and Vila Mariana → *Metrô Paraíso, Ana Rosa, Vila Mariana.*
Southwest of Liberdade, beginning where Avenida Paulista becomes Rua Vergueiro, are the neighbourhoods of Paraíso and Vila Mariana. **Paraíso** is dominated by the hulking dome of the **Catedral Ortodoxa** ① *R Vergueiro 1515, Paraíso, T011-5579 3835, www. catedralortodoxa.com.br, Mon-Fri 0900-1300 and 1500-1800, Sat 1000-1300, Mass at 1015 on Sun, Metrô Paraíso.* The church is modelled on the Hagia Sofia in Istanbul and is one of the largest Antiochian Orthodox churches in the world. Most of the worshippers are Brazilians of Syrian and Lebanese descent. The church of Antioch is one of the five original churches and was founded in Antioch (Turkey) by the apostles Peter and Paul. Its seat is in Damascus, Syria and the current patriarch is His Beatitude Patriarch Ignatius IV (Hazim) of Antioch and all the East.

Vila Mariana is principally a residential neighbourhood abutting Ibirapuera Park. It's home to one of Brazil's few Chinese Buddhist cultural centres, the **Centro Cultural Tzong Kwan** ① *R Rio Grande 490, Vila Mariana, T011-993 483 600 3000, www.tzongkwan.com. br,* which has a small Buddhist temple and offers a selection of Asian cultural activities including Chinese Tai Chi and Kung Fu, Korean Hapkido, Indian yoga and Mahayana Buddhist meditation. The **SESC Vila Mariana** ① *R Pelotas 141, Vila Mariana, T011-5080 3000, www.sescsp.org.br, daily 1000-2000,* is a cultural centre with a swimming pool, internet, a gym and a concert hall which hosts some of the best small acts in São Paulo. From Metrô Ana Rosa, it's a 10-minute walk south of Ana Rosa, east along Avenida Cnso Rodrigues Alves, right onto Rua Humberto I (after 500 m) and left onto Pelotas (after 200 m).

Late 2012 saw the inauguration of the São Paulo showroom of the cutting-edge British contemporary art gallery **White Cube** ① *R Agostinho Rodrigues Filho 550, Vila Mariana, T011-4329 4474, www.whitecube.com,* with the first Latin American solo show by Tracy Emin. The gallery represents leading British artists such as Damien Hirst and Antony Gormley, who will exhibit in São Paulo. Brazilian artists are in turn set to have their work shown at White Cube in London and at the gallery's branch in Hong Kong.

Parque do Ibirapuera

ⓘ *Entrance on Av Pedro Álvares Cabral, T011-5573 4180, www.parquedo ibirapuera.com, daily 0500-2400, free, unsafe after dark. Metrô Ana Rosa is a 15-min walk east of the park: turn right out of the station and walk due west along Av Conselheiro Rodrigo Alves, continue onto Av Dante Pazzanese which comes to the Av 23 de Maio urban freeway, the park sits in front of you on the other side of the road and can be reached via a footbridge 200 m to the right in front of the new MAC gallery (still known as the Detran building); alternatively bus 5164-21 (marked Cidade Leonor, direção Parque do Ibirapuera) leaves every 30 mins from Metrô Santa Cruz for Ibirapuera; any bus to DETRAN (labelled in huge letters) stops opposite Ibirapuera. Lines include 175T-10, 477U-10 and 675N-10. Metrô Ibirapuera, which will stop outside the Ibirapuera shopping mall is under construction. It will be a 20-min walk from the park.*

The park was designed by architect Oscar Niemeyer and landscape artist Roberto Burle Marx for the city's fourth centenary in 1954. It is the largest of the very few green spaces in central São Paulo and its shady woodlands, lawns and lakes offer a breath of fresher air in a city that has only 4.6 sq m of vegetation per inhabitant. The park is also home to a number of museums and monuments and some striking Oscar Niemeyer buildings that were designed in the 1950s but which have only been constructed in the last five years. These include the **Pavilhão Lucas Nogueira Garcez**, most commonly referred to as the **Oca** ⓘ *Portão 3, open for exhibitions*, a brilliant white, polished concrete dome, built in homage to an indigenous Brazilian roundhouse. It stages major international art exhibitions (see the Ibirapuera website for what's on). Next to it is the **Auditório Ibirapuera** ⓘ *Portão 3, www. auditorioibirapuera.com.br*, a concert hall shaped like a giant wedge. The **Fundação Bienal** ⓘ *Portão 3, http://bienalsaopaulo.globo.com, open for exhibitions*, are also by Niemeyer and house the city's flagship fashion and art events: the twice yearly **São Paulo fashion week** and the **Art Biennial**, the most important events of their kind in the southern hemisphere.

A **sculpture garden** separates the Bienal from the Oca; this garden is watched over by the **Museu de Arte Moderna** (**MAM**) ⓘ *Portão 3, T011-5085 1300, www.mam.org.br, Tue-Sun 1000-1730 (ticket office closes at 1700), US$3, free on Sun*. This small museum, with a giant mural outside by Os Gêmeos, showcases the best Brazilian contemporary art in temporary exhibitions. There is always something worth seeing and the gallery has an excellent buffet restaurant and gift shop. MAM is linked by a covered walkway to the **Museu Afro-Brasil** ⓘ *Portão 10, T011-3320 8900, www.museuafrobrasil.com.br, Tue-Sun 1000-1700, US$5*, which lies inside Niemeyer's spectacular stilted **Pavilhão Manoel da Nobrega** building and devotes more than 12,000 sq m to a celebration of black Brazilian culture. Events include regular films, music, dance, and theatrical events and there is an archive of over 5000 photographs, paintings, ritual objects and artefacts which include the bisected hull of a slaving ship showing the conditions under which Africans were brought to Brazil.

A few hundred metres to the west of here, on the shores of the artificial lake, the **Planetário e Museu de Astronomia Professor Aristóteles Orsini** (**Planetarium**) ⓘ *Portão 10, T011-5575 5206, www.prefeitura.sp.gov.br/astronomia, Sat and Sun 1200-1800, US$5*, was restored in 2006 with a new projection ceiling and state-of-the-art Star Master projection equipment by Carl Zeiss, and is now one of the most impressive in Latin America. Shows are in Portuguese.

Less than 100 m to the south, is the **Pavilhão Japonês** ⓘ *Portão 10, T011-5081 7296, http://www.bunkyo.bunkyonet.org.br Wed, Sat, Sun and holidays 1300-1700, free except for exhibitions*. The building is inspired by the historic Kyoto summer residence of Japanese emperors, the Palácio Katsura, which was built 1620-1624 under the Tokugawa shogunate.

The pavilion itself was built in Japan under the supervision of Sutemi Horiguchi – one of 20th-century Japan's foremost modern architects, responsible for buildings including the Machinery Hall, which he designed for the Tokyo Peace Exhibition of 1922. The pavilion is built in strict adherence to Japanese aesthetic principles and re-assembled next to the park's largest lake (which has illuminated fountain displays on weekday evenings). The pavilion on the lower floor has an exhibition space devoted to Japanese-Brazilian culture and has a traditional Japanese tearoom upstairs.

The park also has a running track, **Pista de Cooper** (with pit stops for exercise with pull-up bars, weight machines and chunky wooden dumbells), football pitches and hosts regular open-air concerts on Sundays. Those seeking something quieter on a Sunday can borrow a book from the portable library and read it in the shade of the **Bosque da Leitura** or 'reading wood'. Bicycles can be hired in the park (US$3 per hour) and there are dozens of small snack vendors and café-restaurants.

Ibirapuera also has a few monuments of note. **O Monumento as Bandeiras**, which sits on the northern edge of the park, is a brutalist tribute to the marauding and bloodthirsty slave traders, or *bandeirantes*, who opened up the interior of Brazil. It was created by Brazil's foremost 20th-century sculptor, Victor Brecheret. The **Obelisco aos Héroes de 32**, on the eastern edge of the park, is a monumental Cleopatra's needle built in honour of the Paulistano rebels who died in 1932 when the dictator Getúlio Vargas crushed resistance to his Estado Novo regime. Above the rushing Sena Madureira urban highway – where it thunders into the tunnel which passes beneath the park – is **Velocidade, Alma e Emoção** (Speed, Soul and Emotion), a bronze tribute to one of São Paulo's favourite sons, the Formula One driver **Ayrton Senna**, by local artist Melinda Garcia.

A bridge leads across the 16-lane Avenida 23 de Maio urban highway in the southeast corner of the park near Portao 4 to the former DETRAN building, which is a giant oblong on stilts by Oscar Niemeyer. Until 2007 it was home to the state transit authority. In late 2012 after a refurbishment costing US$38 million, it reopened as the new central São Paulo wing of the **Museu de Arte Contemporanea de São Paulo (MAC)** ① *Av Pedro Álvares Cabral 1301, T011-5573 9932, Tue-Sun 1000-1800*. At present only the ground floor functions as a gallery, showing sculptures by the likes of Henry Moore. All the other galleries (and the vast archive of important works due to be shown within them by the likes of Picasso, Chagal, De Chirico and Tarsila do Amaral) remain off limits. This is due to a failure on the part of the Secretaria de Estado da Cultura to install adequate security.

Itaim Bibi, Vila Olímpia and Moema → *Metrô Faria Lima and Moema (both under construction), CPTM Vila Olímpia and Cidade Jardim.*
Business mixes with pleasure in these plush neighbourhoods south of Jardins and near Ibirapuera park. By day they are filled with office workers; by night, especially at weekends, hundreds of street bars and clubs are busy with partying Paulistano professionals.

Further afield → *For listings, see pages 48-68.*

Brooklin and the New Business District → *CPTM Brooklin, Metrô Brooklin (under construction).*
Brooklin's Avenida Engenheiro Luís Carlos Berrini has taken over from Avenida Paulista as the business centre of the new São Paulo. Many of the larger companies, banks and international corporations now have their South American headquarters here, making this a likely centre of operations for those visiting the city for a work trip.

Parque do Estado

This large park, housing the botanical and zoological gardens, is 15 km south of the centre at **Água Funda**. The **Jardim Botânico** ① *Av Miguel Estefano s/n, Água Funda, T011-5073 6300, www.ibot.sp.gov.br, Tue-Sun 0900-1700, US$1.50, Metrô São Judas and then bus 4742 marked Jardim Climax, or taxi from Metrô Jabaquara (US$10)*, has a vast garden esplanade surrounded by magnificent stone porches, with lakes and trees and places for picnics, and a very fine orchid farm worth seeing during the flowering season (November to December). More than 19,000 different kinds of orchids are cultivated. There are orchid exhibitions in April and November. The astronomical **observatory** nearby is open to the public on Thursday afternoons. Howler monkeys, guans and toco toucans can be seen here towards the end of the day.

The **Jardim Zoológico** ① *Av Miguel Estefano 4241, Água Funda, T011-5073 0811, www.zoologico.com.br, Tue-Sun 0900-1700, US$9, US$3.50 children, under 4s free, Metrô Jabaquara (shuttle from the metrô station to the zoo, US$2.50 when bought with a ticket to the zoo at the metrô ticket office in Jabaquara)*, is the biggest zoo in the country and claims that it is the fourth biggest in the world, with 3200 animals, including large international mammals and many rare and endangered Brazilian species. These include jaguar, puma (in small enclosures), Spix's macaw (which is extinct in the wild), Lear's macaw (which is critically endangered), Harpy eagle, bush dog and maned wolf.

Butantã and the Cidade Universitária

Instituto Butantã/Butantã Institute and Venomous Animal Museum ① *Av Dr Vital Brasil 1500, T011-2627 9536, Tue-Sun 0900-1645, www.butantan.gov.br, US$3, children US$1.25, under 7s free, Metrô Butantã*, on the university campus is one of the most popular tourist attractions in São Paulo. The Butantã Institute was founded at the start of the 20th century when São Paulo's governors looked to Brazilian scientists after an outbreak of bubonic plague in the port city of Santos. Over the decades, as São Paulo became a booming centre of coffee production, researchers sought vaccines against snake bites to protect coffee harvesters working in the fields. The snakes are in pits and a large walk-through vivarium which also houses venomous spiders and scorpions. There is also a well-displayed, modern microbiology museum at the institute. The animals are milked for their venom six times a day and the antidotes have greatly reduced deaths from snakebite in Brazil. The centre also deals with spider and scorpion venom, has a small hospital and is a biomedical research institute responsible for producing about 90% of vaccines used in Brazil, including recent vaccines against H1N1 flu. Recent years have seen the institute invest in the hunt for natural vaccines in the Amazon rainforest. Visitors are not likely to see the venom being milked, but there is a museum of poisonous animals, which is well organized and educational, with explanations in Portuguese and English. The institute suffered a serious fire in May 2010, with the loss of the 85,000-strong preserved snake collection and 450,000 spider and scorpion specimens. It was the largest such collection in the world. The vivarium and public museum areas of the institute were not affected.

In the Prédio Novo da Reitoria, the **Museu de Arte Contemporânea (MAC)** ① *T011-3091 3039, www.mac.usp.br, Mon-Fri 1000-1800, Sun 1000-1600, free, Metrô Butantã*, has an important and beautifully presented collection of Brazilian and European modern art, with pieces by Braque, Picasso, Modigliani, Matisse and Tarsila do Amaral. The gallery has a further wing next to Ibirapuera Park (see page 42). Also in the university is the **Museu de Arqueologia e Etnologia (MAE)** ① *R Reitoria 1466, T011-3812 4001*, with an ill-kept collection of Amazonian and ancient Mediterranean material.

On the west bank of the Rio Pinheiros, just southeast of the campus, is the palatial Jockey Club de São Paulo ① *Av Lineu de Paula Machado 1263, T011-3811 7799, www. jockeysp.com.br; take a bus from Praça da República*, a racecourse in the Cidade Jardim area. Race meetings are held on Monday and Thursday at 1930 and on weekends at 1430.

Ipiranga and the Parque da Independência

① *To get to the park, take the* metrô *to Alto do Ipiranga station, walk 30 m east to Av Dr Gentil de Moura and catch bus 478P-10 Sacoma-Pompeia to Av Nazaré (4 stops), get off and walk north for 200 m to the Parque da Independência. It is also possible to catch the CPTM to Ipiranga station and walk east across the Viaduto Pacheco Chaves bridge and along R dos Patriotas (for 1 km). Bus No 478P (Ipiranga–Pompéia for return) runs from Metrô Ana Rosa and bus No 4612 from the Praça da República.*

The **Parque da Independência**, on Avenida Nazaré, is a large, formal park on the site where Brazilian independence was declared. It is littered with monuments to independence and Brazil's early imperial past. It is watched over by a faux-French chateau, recalling Versailles, which houses one of the city's largest museums. Dominating the northern end of the park is the **Monumento à Independência**, depicting the first Brazilian emperor, Dom Pedro, brandishing a furled flag and uttering his famous 'Grito de Ipiranga' (Ipiranga cry) – 'Independence or Death!', which declared Brazil's separation from Portugal. Beneath the monument is the **Imperial Chapel** ① *Tue-Sun 1300-1700*, containing Dom Pedro and Empress Leopoldina's tomb. The monument was built to commemorate the centenary of Independence in 1922. The **Casa do Grito** ① *Tue-Sun 0930-1700*, is a replica of the tiny house where Dom Pedro I spent the night before uttering his grito. At that time, Ipiranga was outside the city's boundaries, in a wooded area on the main trade route between Santos and São Paulo. Bricks were made here from a local red clay, known as ipiranga in the Tupi language. This clay has given its name to the surrounding neighbourhood.

The **Museu Paulista** ① *T011-2065 8000, www.mp.usp.br, Tue-Sun 0900-1700, US$3, free on the 1st Sun of every month*, is housed in a huge palace at the top of the park. The original building, later altered, was the first monument to Independence. The museum contains old maps, traditional furniture, collections of old coins, religious art and rare documents, and has a department of indigenous ethnology. Behind the museum is the **Horto Botânico/ Ipiranga Botanical Garden** ① *Tue-Sun 0900-1700*, and the **Jardim Francês**, designed as a garden for plant study, now a recreational area. There is a light and sound show on Brazilian history in the park on Wednesday, Friday and Saturday at 2030.

Mooca, Brás and the Zona Leste

São Paulo's Zona Leste is predominantly a blue collar residential region that becomes progressively poorer the farther from the centre you go, eventually tailing off into vast sprawling *favelas*, such as the Favela do Sapo, on the city's outskirts. Most of the city's domestic workers live here (or in similar marginalized communities such as Paraisópolis in the north), near Ipiranga or Jardim Angela (in Capão Redondo in the city's far south).

One of the few well-to-do neighbourhoods, **Mooca**, is home to the impressive **Museu da Imigração do Estado de São Paulo** ① *R Visconde de Parnaíba 1316, Mooca, T011-3311 7700, www.memorialdoimigrante.org.br, Tue-Sun 1000-1700, US$4, Metrô Bresser, from where an original 1912 tram runs to and from the museum during opening hours*, dedicated to the hundreds of thousands of Europeans who flooded into the country from the late 19th century to harvest coffee and work the plantations. Most came on government-funded programmes similar to the one pound package which populated Australia with

British emigrants in the 20th century. As many as 10,000 Germans, Italians, Ukrainians, Spanish and Portuguese came to Brazil every day from the arrival of the first boat in 1870 until the last at beginning of Second World War. They were housed and fed for free for eight days before being left to the mercy of often ruthless landowners who had only recently abandoned slavery. Treatment was often so bad that adverts were run in Europe advising people not to leave for Brazil. This museum tells little of that story, or of the African-Brazilians who were denied work in favour of Europeans, in what amounted to a kind of employment apartheid, but there are fascinating exhibits on life in the early 20th-century Brazil and the lifestyle of the first immigrants. A **railway station** next to the museum offers 800-m-long rides on two North American steam trains of the former Central do Brasil rail – a Pacific 353 and a Baldwin 0-6-0, which run on weekends. Both pull authentic 19th- or early 20th-century wooden carriages. As this book went to press in 2013 the museum was closed for extensive refurbishment. Check the website for the latest on opening.

The neighbourhood of **Brás**, which is contiguous to Mooca, is home to the city's science, natural history and technology museum **Catavento Cultural e Educacional** ① *Palácio das Indústrias s/n, Parque Dom Pedro II, T011-3315 0051; Metrô Dom Pedro II or São Bento; or by bus to the terminal de ônibus Parque Dom Pedro II, see www.sptrans.com.br for details on bus lines*, housed in a huge eclectic former industrial mansion. Galleries are themed as Universe, Life, Manufacturing and Society and exhibits and displays are aimed resolutely at the young, aiming to stimulate their interest in all things scientific, from biology through to manufacturing technology. The interactive displays are engaging and the museum is a popular with school trips so can be crowded on weekday mornings.

The suburbs → *For listings, see pages 48-68.*

Parque Burle Marx

① *Av Dona Helena Pereira de Moraes 200, Morumbi, daily 0700-1900, CPTM Estação Granja Julieta or Metrô Santo Amara or taxi (US$10); there are no buses and it's unsafe to walk*, was designed by the famous landscape designer Burle Marx. It is the only place in the city where you can walk along trails in the Mata Atlântica (Atlantic rainforest), but it is unsafe after dark as it lies very close to Paraisópolis, the second largest *favela* in São Paulo (after Heliópolis).

Interlagos

The **Brazilian Grand Prix** is staged at the **Autódromo de Interlagos** ① *Av Senador Teotônio Vilela 261, Interlagos, T011-5666 8822, www.autodromointerlagos.com*, overlooking a vast artificial lake set in remnant forest in the far southeast of the city. There are races all year round; details can be found on the website. For information on the Brazilian Grand Prix see box, page 61.

Beyond Interlagos, São Paulo merges with the beautiful misty mountains and cloud forests of the Serra do Mar, its concrete gradually giving way to fresh air and trees. At **Parelheiros** there is access to the Mata Atlântica Atlantic coastal rain, cloud and elfin forests in and around the 315,000-ha **Parque Estadual Serra do Mar**, a state park and protected area stretching through the *serra* all the way to Rio and offering wonderful day hiking and excellent birdwatching. Maned wolf and ocelot still live in the area and brown capuchin monkeys are a common sight. The area can be visited with **Trip on Jeep.**

Paranapiacaba

ⓘ *Suburban trains leave from the Estação da Luz every 15 mins for Rio Grande da Serra (Line 10 – the turquoise line), US$2.50, 55 mins. From Rio Grande da Serra station, bus No 424 runs to Paranapiacaba hourly during the week, every 30 mins at weekends. The journey is around 1 hr. An Expresso Turístico tourist train (with an authentic 1950s locomotive and carriages) leaves Luz at 0830 for Paranapiacaba, returning at 1630, US$18; see www.cptm.sp.gov.br/e_operacao/exprtur/parana.asp for the latest details.*

This tiny 19th-century town, nestled in the cloudforest of the Serra do Mar about 50 km southeast of São Paulo, was built by English railway workers who constructed the São Paulo–Santos railway. Almost all of the houses are made of wood and many look like they belong in suburban Surrey. There is a small railway museum and a handful of little *pousadas* and restaurants. It is easily visited in a day trip from São Paulo.

Serra da Cantareira

Whilst the Serra do Mar mountains bring greenery to São Paulo's southern edges, the Serra da Cantareira provides fresh air and forest to its north. Unlike the Serra do Mar, the Serra da Cantareira is cut by small roads, and at weekends Paulistanos traditionally love to slip on their Timberlands, climb into the car and drive through the hills in search of nothing wilder than a steakhouse. But there are trails and, if you're prepared to walk, you can get lost in some semi-wilderness. It's best to go with a guide through a local company such as **Tropico** ⓘ *www.tropico.tur.br*, or **Trip on Jeep**, which offers guided hikes to rushing rainforest waterfalls with glassy plunge pools, and to boulder mountains with sweeping views of the skyscraper city over a canopy of trees.

Embu das Artes

This colonial town, 28 km southwest of São Paulo, has become a centre for artists and craftsmen and has a wealth of arts, crafts, furniture and rustic design shops and dozens of restaurants serving hearty Brazilian fare. The pedestrianized streets of the tiny town centre cluster around a little Jesuit church with a **Sacred Art Museum** ⓘ *Largo dos Jesuítas 67, T011-4704 2654, Tue-Sun 1000-1200 and 1400-1800*, crowning a hill. Many of the old houses are brightly coloured and a busy arts and crafts market fills the town centre at the weekend when Embu fills with visitors from São Paulo. While Embu is a delight it became known internationally in the latter half of the 20th century as the final resting place of the notorious SS physician from Auschwitz Josef Mengele who was buried here under his assumed name, Wolfgang Gerhard. The body has since been exhumed.

São Paulo city listings

For hotel and restaurant price codes and other relevant information, see pages 8-11.

● Where to stay

São Paulo has the best hotels in Latin America and by far the best city hotels in Brazil. There are designer hotels that Ian Shrager would be proud of, including business towers that combine all the requisite facilities with an almost personal touch. However, rooms are expensive and while there are some reasonable budget options they are not in the best locations. Sampa (as São Paulo is affectionately known) is a place where you have to spend money to enjoy yourself. The best places to stay are **Jardins** (the most affluent area) and on and around **Av Paulista** (close to one of the business centres). Backpackers should consider **Vila Madalena** – a lively nightlife centre with a recently opened hostel. Business travellers will find good hotels in **Faria Lima** and **Av Luís Carlos Berrini** (in the new centre in the south of the city). Some of the better hostels are in seemingly random locations and there are cheap options in the seedy centre, which is an undesirable place to be at night.

Centro Histórico *p25, map p28*
Metrô República and Anhangabaú
The city centre is very busy during the day but decidedly sketchy after dark. Consider taking a cab from your hotel door and be extra careful if you resolve to walk around. Be sure to book rooms on upper floors of hotels, preferably not facing the street, for a quiet night in the city centre.
$$$ Marabá, Av Ipiranga 757, T011-2137 9500, www.hotelmaraba.com.br. By far the best small hotel in the city centre, this newly refurbished building has colourful, well-appointed modern rooms with concessions to boutique hotel design.

$$$ Novotel Jaraguá Convention, R Martins Fontes 71, T011-2802 7000, www.novotel.com. This freshly refurbished chain hotel with Wi-Fi in all rooms is the only business hotel of quality in the old centre.
$$ Formule 1, Av São João 1140, Centre, just off Praça da República, T011-2878 6400, www.accor.com.br. 5 mins' walk from Metrô República. You'll feel like you're part of a process rather than a guest at this tall chain hotel tower. However, the modern, functional and anonymous little a/c boxes are spick and span and come with en suites, TVs, work places and space for 3 people.
$$ Itamarati, Av Dr Vieira de Carvalho 150, T011-3474 4133, www.hotelitamarati.com.br. This long-standing cheapie is popular with budget travellers and represents the best value for money of any hotel in the city centre.

Avenida Paulista and Jardins *p35 and p38, map p36*
Metrô Brigadeiro, Trianon MASP, Consolação and Oscar Freire (under construction)
These plush neighbourhoods are among the safest in the city and offer easy walking access to São Paulo's finest restaurants, cafés, and shops. Those close to Av Paulista are a stroll from one of a string of *metrô* stations. A new *metrô* is under construction at R Oscar Freire (due late 2014) in the heart of Jardins.
$$$$ Emiliano, R Oscar Freire 384, T011-3069 4369, www.emiliano.com.br. Together with the **Fasano** and **Unique**, these are best suites in the city: bright, light and beautifully designed with attention to every detail. No pool but a relaxing small spa. Excellent Italian restaurant, location and service.
$$$$ Fasano, R Vittorio Fasano 88, T011-3896 4077, www.fasano.com.br. One of the world's great hotels. There's a fabulous pool, a spa and the best formal haute cuisine restaurant in Brazil. The lobby bar is

a wonderful place to arrange a meeting. Excellent position in Jardins.

$$$$ George V, R Jose Maria Lisboa 1000, T011-3088 9822, www.george-v.com.br. This tower block in the heart of Jardins offers some of the largest apartments in central São Paulo covering 60-180 sq m. Living areas and bedrooms have flatscreen TVs, fully equipped kitchens (with dishwashers and washing machines), huge marble bathrooms, closets and comprehensive business services.

$$$$ L'Hotel, Av Campinas 266, T011-2183 0500, www.lhotel.com.br. Part of the **Leading Hotels of the World** group, with a series of suites decorated with mock-European paintings and patterned wallpaper, in emulation of the classic hotel look of New York's Upper East Side. The St Regis this is not, but it's comfortable, intimate, offers good, discreet service and a respectable French restaurant. A convenient base for Paulista.

$$$$ Renaissance, Alameda Santos 2233 (at Haddock Lobo), T011-3069 2233, www.marriott.com. This tall tower designed by Ruy Ohtake is the best business hotel around Av Paulista, with spacious and well-appointed rooms (the best with wonderful city views), a good spa, gym, pool and 2 squash courts.

$$$$ Tivoli Mofarrej, R Alameda Santos 1437, Jardins, T011-3146 5900, www.tivoli hotels. com. A selection of plush, modern carpeted suites and smaller rooms, the best of which are on the upper storeys and have superb city views. The hotel has the best spa in the city – run by the **Banyan Tree** group.

$$$$ Unique, Av Brigadeiro Luís Antônio 4700, Jardim Paulista, T011-3055 4700, www.hotelunique.com. The most ostentatiously designed hotel in the country: an enormous half moon on concrete uprights with curving floors, circular windows with a beautiful use of space and light. The bar on the top floor is São Paulo's answer to the LA Sky Bar and is filled with the beautiful and famous.

$$$ Golden Tulip Park Plaza, Alameda Lorena 360, T011-2627 6000, www.golden tulippark plaza.com. Modern tower hotel with a pool, spa, business centre, gym, also has freshly re-vamped apartments of some 30 sq m. All have a clean, modern look with wood panel floors, fitted wardrobes, good-sized workplaces and firm beds.

$$$ Transamérica Ópera, Alameda Lorena 1748, T011-3062 2666, www.transamericaflats.com.br. Newly decorated but elegant and well-maintained modern flats of 42 sq m in a tower between the heart of Jardins and Av Paulista. Choose a room above floor 15 for quietness and views.

$$$-$$ Pousada Dona Zilah, Alameda Franca 1621, Jardim Paulista, T011-3062 1444, www.zilah.com. Little *pousada* in a renovated colonial house with plain but well-maintained rooms and common areas decorated with a personal touch.

$$ Estan Plaza, Alameda Jau 497, Jardins, T011-3016 0000, www.estanplaza.com.br. Well-kept, simple and pocket-sized rooms in a well-situated tower block close to both the restaurants of Jardins and Av Paulista. Rooms are at a similar price to hostel doubles making this excellent value.

$$ Ibis São Paulo Paulista, Av Paulista 2355, T011-3523 3000, www.accorhotels.com.br. Great value. Modern, business-standard rooms with a/c in a tower right on Av Paulista. Cheaper at weekends. Online reservations.

$$ Paulista Garden, Alameda Lorena 21, T011-3885 8498, www.paulistagardenhotel.com.br. Very simple, uninspiring hotel, but the location is excellent.

Vila Madalena and Pinheiros *p39, map p26*

Metrô Vila Madalena and Fradique Coutinho (the latter under construction)

These are great neighbourhoods to stay in, with a wealth of little shops, café-restaurants, bars and nightclubs. The *metrô* station is 10 mins' walk from most of the action but there are fast subway trains from here to the city centre and connections to Paulista and the *rodoviária*. There are only 3 accommodation options for now, but more are sure to follow.

$$ Casa Club, R Mourato Coelho 973, T011-3798 0051, www.casaclub.com.br. There are only 4 rooms in this tiny hostel and whilst they're all dorms they can be booked as private rooms. One is for women only. The hostel began life as a bar and the after-hours party atmosphere remains to this day, so it's not an option for those craving peace or privacy. Free Wi-Fi and a restaurant.

$$ Guest 607, R João Moura 607, Pinheiros, T011-2619 6007, www.guest607.com.br. This very simple but colourfully painted little guesthouse, a stroll from the Benedito Calixto weekend market, offers a bright and cosy stay, albeit it in tiny rooms. There's a decent food in the little café-restaurant, free Wi-Fi and the rooms are about as cheap as it gets in São Paulo outside a hostel dorm.

$$ Sampa Hostel, R Girassol 519, T011-3031 6779, www.hostelsampa.com.br. This small hostel is in the heart of Vila Madalena, close to shops, cafés and bars. The 2 private rooms fill up quickly so book ahead, the rest of the accommodation is in dorms. All are fan cooled. Prices include breakfast. Wi-Fi is available throughout the hostel at a flat one-off US$3.50 fee.

South of the centre *p40, map p26*
Metrô Anhangabaú, Liberdade, Paraíso and Vergueiro

$$$-$$ Paradiso Hostel, R Chuí 195, T011-9981 18633, www.paradisohostel. com. Rooms in 2 modest townhouses in a quiet street just behind the Orthodox cathedral. All are spacious, clean and quiet and come with free Wi-Fi. While there is no breakfast there's a very good padaria round the corner. Service can be a lackadaisical.

$$ 3 Dogs Hostel, R Cel Artur Godoi 51, Vila Mariana, T011-2359 8222, www.3dogshostel.com.br. Double rooms and dorms, breakfast and bed linen included, with garden and free Wi-Fi.

$$ Formule 1, R Vergueiro 1571, T011-5085 5699, www.accorhotels.com.br. Great-value business-style hotel, with a/c apartments big enough for 3 (making this an $ option for those in a group). Right next to Metrô Paraíso, in a safe area.

$$ Pousada dos Franceses, R dos Franceses 100, Bela Vista, T011-3288 1592, www.pousadadosfranceses.com.br. Price per person. A plain little *pousada* with an attractive garden, a BBQ area, laundry facilities, dorms, doubles and singles. 10 mins' walk from Metrô Brigadeiro. Free internet, TV room and breakfast included.

$$ Praça da Árvore IYHA, R Pageú 266, Saúde, T011-5071 5148, www.spalbergue. com.br. This pleasant little hostel with friendly, helpful and English-speaking staff, lies 2 mins from the Metrô Praça do Arvore – some 20 mins' ride from the city centre. It is situated in a large residential house in a quiet back street. Facilities include a kitchen, laundry and internet service.

$$ Vergueiro Hostel, R Vergueiro 434, Liberdade, T011-2649 1323, www.hostel vergueiro.com. Simple eggshell blue or burnt ochre rooms with parquet wood or square-tile floors, some of which have balconies.

Itaim Bibi, Vila Olímpia and Moema
p43, map p26
Metrô Faria Lima, CPTM Vila Olímpia and Cidade Jardim and Faria Lima and Moema (the latter due to open in 2015)

$$$$ Blue Tree Towers, Av Brigadeiro Faria Lima 3989, Vila Olímpia, T011-3896 7544, www.bluetree.com.br. Modern business hotel with discreetly designed rooms and excellent service.

Brooklin and the New Business District *p43, map p26*
Metrô Brooklin (due to open in 2015)
This is São Paulo's new business capital. Most hotels are to be found on Av Brigadeiro Faria Lima and Av Luís Carlos Berrini.

$$$$ Grand Hyatt São Paulo, Av das Nações Unidas 13301, T011-2838 1234,

www.saopaulo.hyatt.com. A superb business
hotel close to Av Luís Carlos Berrini, which
successfully fuses corporate efficiency and
requisite services with designer cool. Spa,
pool, state-of-the-art business centre and
marvellous views from the upper-floor suites.
$$$$ Hilton São Paulo, Av das Nações
Unidas 12901, T011-2845 0000, www.
hilton.com. This tall tower in the heart of
the new business district overlooks the new
Octavio Frias de Oliveira twin suspension
bridge and boasts a vast marble lobby with
Wi-Fi access (none in rooms), business and
conference facilities and a 24-hr spa. Rooms
come with marble bathrooms, an office
workstation with broadband and sweeping
city views from the upper floors.

The suburbs *p46, map p26*
Shuttle services from Unique Hotel in São Paulo
city (see page 49).
$$$$ Unique Garden Spa, Estrada 3500,
Serra da Cantareira, T011-4486 8724, www.
uniquegarden.com.br. The über-cool style
of hotel **Unique** (see page 49) transposed
into a natural setting of the Serra da
Cantareira subtropical forest, 40 mins north
of São Paulo. The buildings are a series of
Frank Lloyd Wright-inspired post-modernist
bungalows. Wonderful spa treatments.

🍴 Restaurants

Those on a budget can eat to their
stomach's content in per kg places or,
if looking for cheaper still, in *padarias*
(bakeries). There is one of these on almost
every corner; they all serve sandwiches
such as *Misto Quentes*, *Beirutes* and
Americanos – delicious Brazilian burgers
made from decent meat and served with
ham, egg, cheese or salad. They always have
good coffee, juices, cakes and *almoços* (set
lunches) for a very economical price. Most
have a designated seating area, either at
the *padaria* bar or in an adjacent room; you
aren't expected to eat on your feet as you
are in Rio. Restaurants in São Paulo are safe

on the stomach. Juices are made
with mineral or filtered water.

Centro Histórico *p25, map p28*
Metrô Luz, República, São Bento, Anhangabaú, Sé
You are never far from a café or restaurant
in the city centre and Luz. The Pinacoteca
galleries, the Centro Culutral Banco do Brasil
and the Pátio de Colégio all have decent
cafés, and there are dozens in the streets
around the Mosteiro São Bento and the
Teatro Municipal. Most tend to be open
during lunchtime only and there are many
per kilo options and *padarias*.
$$$ Terraço Italia, Av Ipiranga 344, T011-
3257 6566. An overpriced Italian restaurant,
with stodgy pasta and the best views in
the city of any dining room in São Paulo.
Come for a coffee only, although there's a
minimum charge of some US$12.50.
$$ Efigênia Café e Bar, Largo São Bento
s/n, T011-3311 8800. A perfect pit-stop while
on a tour of the city centre. Sit and watch
the city go by from one of the tables nested
under the Viaduto Santa Ifigênia bridge
whilst lunching on a decent-value buffet of
hot and cold plates of Brazilian standards.
$$-$ Ponto Chic, Largo do Paiçandu 27,
T011-3222 6528, www.pontochic.com.
br. Paulistanos rave about this rather
unprepossessing little corner café in the
heart of the city. A slice of Brazilian culinary
history, the Bauru sandwich was born here
in 1922. A bronze bust of Casemiro Pinto
Neto (who apparently first conceived the
ground-breaking idea of combining cheese,
salad and roast beef in a French bread roll)
adorns the back wall. The sandwich itself
has a page of the menu devoted to its
history, but arrives with little ceremony on
a plain white plate, overflowing with gooey
cheese and thick with fine-cut beef.

Luz *p33, map p26*
$$-$ Café da Pinacoteca, Pinacoteca
Museum, Praça da Luz 2, Luz, T011-
3326 0350. This Portuguese-style café with
marble floors and mahogany balconies

overlooks the Parque da Luz on the basement floor of the Pinacoteca gallery. It serves great coffee, sandwiches, snacks and cakes. There is also a café of similar quality in the Estação Pinacoteca gallery.

Barra Funda and Higienópolis *p34, map p26*

$$$ Carlota, R Sergipe 753, Higienópolis, T011-3661 8670, www.carlota.com.br. Chef Carla Pernambuco was a pioneer of fine dining in Brazil when she first opened her restaurant in the mid-1990s. Her recipe of unpretentious, homey surrounds, warm service and Brazilian and Mediterranean fusion cooking has been copied by numerous others in São Paulo. Dishes include fillet of grouper with plantain banana purée and fresh asparagus.

$$$ Corrientes 348, R Bahia, 364, Higienópolis, T011-3849 0348, www.restaurante348.com.br. A newly opened branch of the superb Vila Olimpia Argentinian meat restaurant (see page 55) which has long held the reputation for having the best steaks in the city. Excellent wine list.

Avenida Paulista and Consolação
p35 and p37, map p36
Metrô Consolação, Trianon-MASP, Brigadeiro
Restaurants in this area lie along the course of Av Paulista or in the up-and-coming nightlife are of Consolação to the north. Jardins lies within easy access to the south.

$$$ Spot, Av Ministro Rocha Azevedo 72, T011-3284 6131, www.restaurantespot.com.br. This chic São Paulo take on an American diner has been a favourite before-and-after club spot for fashionable Paulistanos for more than a decade.

$$$-$$ Tordesilhas, R Bela Cintra 465, Consolação, T011-3107 7444, www.tordesilhas.com. This homey restaurant with shady plants, polished floor tiles and plenty of natural light feels as informal as a barbecue in the back yard. Cooking, likewise, is Brazilian home comfort fare, albeit with

a contemporary creative touch – delicious *tutu à mineira* (pork with puréed beans and *farofa*), *moquecas* (including a plantain banana option for vegetarians), and for dessert dishes like *cupuaçu* crème brûlée.

$$ Restaurante do MASP, Av Paulista 1578, T011-3253 2829 (see page 35). This bright, hospital-clean buffet restaurant in the basement of the museum serves good-value comfort food such as lasagne and stroganoff, accompanied by salad from the buffet bar.

$$-$ America, Av Paulista 2295, Consolação, T011-3067 4424, www.americaburger.com.br. This immensely popular a/c tribute to the New York diner and the North American burger is a great choice for families.

$$-$ Fran's Café, Av Paulista 358, and all over the city. Open 24 hrs. Coffee chain serving aromatic, strong, richly flavoured coffee at a civilized temperature and in European-sized china cups, together with a menu of light eats.

Jardins *p38, map p36*
Metrô Oscar Freire, Consolação or Trianon-MASP 10 mins' walk
Most of the city's fine dining restaurants lie in this upmarket grid of streets to the south of Av Paulista.

$$$ Casa Nero, Al Lorena 2101, Jardins, T011-3081 2966, www.casanero.com.br. The chicest steakhouse in São Paulo with a mood-lit interior and choice-cuts of Brazilian and Argentine meat grilled or barbecued and served to the some of the city's most fashionably dressed.

$$$ Dalva e Dito, R Padre Joao Manoel 1115, T011-3064 6183, www.dalvaedito.com.br. Brazil's most internationally vaunted chef, Alex Atala, opened his new dining room in 2009 to serve Brazilian home cooking with a gourmet twist. Dishes include roast pork with puréed potato and catfish with aromatic capim-santo grass from the plains of the Brazilian interior.

$$$ D.O.M., R Barão de Capanema 549, T011-3088 0761, www.domrestaurante.com.

br. This has been Jardins' evening 'restaurant of the moment' for almost a decade. The kitchen is run by chef Alex Attala, who has won the coveted *Veja* award several times and currently stands at number 6 on the San Pellegrino 'World's 50 Best Restaurants' list. Contemporary food fuses Brazilian ingredients with French and Italian styles and is served in a large, open, modernist dining room to the sharply dressed.

$$$ Dui, Alameda Franca 1590, T011-2649 7952, www.duirestaurante.com. br. Sumptuous, light Brazilian-Asian-Mediterranean fusion from chef of the moment Bel Coelho who formerly worked in El Celler de Can Roca, one of the world's finest restaurants.

$$$ Eñe, R Dr Mario Ferraz 213, T011-3816 4333, www.enerestaurante.com.br. Brazil's foremost modern Spanish restaurant is helmed by Sergio and Javier Torres Martínez who have worked with Alain Ducasse and Josep Lladonosa of the Escola Arnadí. The *degustação* is a smorgasbord of Spanish and Brazilian-inspired tapas with choices such as breaded mussels and cream of white carrot with tapioca pearls.

$$$ Fasano, Fasano Hotel (see Where to stay, page 48), R Fasano, T011-3062 4000, www.fasano.com.br. The flagship restaurant of the **Fasano** group has long been regarded as the best restaurant for gourmets in São Paulo. It has some stiff competition nowadays, but the menu still offers a delectable choice of modern Italian cooking, from newly inaugurated chef Luca Gozzani (of the **Fasano al Mare** in Rio) and served in a magnificent room where diners have their own low-lit booths and are served by flocks of black-tie waiters. The wine list is exemplary and the dress code formal.

$$$ Figueira Rubaiyat, R Haddock Lobo 1738, T011-3063 1399, www.rubaiyat.com. br. The most interesting of the **Rubaiyat** restaurant group, with steaks prepared by Brazilian chef, Francisco Gameleira. Very lively for lunch on a Sun. Remarkable principally for the space: open walled, light and airy and shaded by a huge tropical fig tree.

$$$ Gero, R Haddock Lobo 1629, T011-3064 0005, www.fasano.com.br. **Fasano**'s version of a French bistro serves pasta and light Italian food in carefully designed, casually chic surrounds.

$$$ Girarrosto, Av Cidade Jardim 60, Jardim Europa, T011-3062 6000, www. girarrosto.com.br. After 13 years of commanding the kitchen at the **Fasano**, Italian-born chef Salvatore Loi finally secured his own restaurant in 2012, where he serves contemporary Italian pastas and risottos including risotto a parmigiana with foie gras, with greens and balsamic vinegar.

$$$ La Tambouille, Av 9 de Julho 5925, Jardim Europa, T011-3079 6277, www. tambouille.com.br. The favourite fusion restaurant of the city's old-money society. Chef Giancarlo Bolla, a native of San Remo in northern Italy, learnt his trade on the Italian Riviera and prepares dishes like fillet of sole with passion fruit sauce served with banana and shrimp farofa.

$$$-$$ Marakuthai, Alameda Itu 1618, T011-3896 5874, www.marakuthai.com.br. A Paulistano take on Indian and Southeast Asian food, with a flavour-filled but very lightly spiced menu from 20-something chef Renata Vanzetto.

$$ A Mineira, Alameda Joaquim Eugenio de Lima 697, T011-3283 2349, www. grupoamineira.com.br. This self-service restaurant offers Minas food by the kilo from a buffet which sizzles in earthenware pots over a woodfire stove.

$$ Santo Grão, R Oscar Freire 413, T011-3082 9969, www.santograo.com.br. This smart café with tables spilling out onto the street is a favourite coffee and cakes or light lunch stop for wealthy society shoppers. The coffee is superb, freshly roasted and comes in a number of varieties.

$$ Sattva, Alameda Itu 1564, T011-3083 6237, www.sattvanatural.com.br. Light vegetarian curries, stir fries, salads, pizzas and pastas all made with organic ingredients. There is a great-value dish of the day lunchtime menu on weekdays and live music most nights.

$$ Tavares, R da Consolação 3212, T011-3062 6026, www.casatavares.com. Good-value breakfasts and *prato feito* lunches (beef/chicken/fish with rice, beans, chips and salad) and a broad à la carte menu ranging from pasta and pizzas to steaks and *bacalhau*.

$ Cheiro Verde, R Peixoto Gomide 1078, Jardins, T011-3262 2640 (lunch only), www.cheiroverderestaurante.com.br. Hearty vegetarian food, such as vegetable crumble in gorgonzola sauce and wholewheat pasta with buffalo mozzarella and sundried tomato.

Vila Madalena and Pinheiros *p39, map p26*

The streets of Vila Madalena are lined with restaurants and cafés, particularly Aspicuelta and Girassol. Most of the bars and clubs serve food too, and some (such as **Grazie o Dio!**) have designated restaurants. Pinheiros has some of the best fine dining restaurants in the city.

$$$ Jun Sakamoto, R Lisboa 55, Pinheiros, T011-3088 6019. Japanese cuisine with a French twist. Superb fresh ingredients, some of it flown in from Asia and the USA. The dishes of choice are the degustation menu and the duck breast teppanyaki.

$$$ Mani, R Joaquim Antunes 210, Pinheiros, T011-3085 4148, www.manimanioca.com.br. Superior light Mediterranean menu, which utilizes Brazilian ingredients and perfectly complements the waistlines of the celebrity crowd. Daniel Redondo and partner Helena Rizzo have worked in Michelin-starred restaurants in Europe and are one of just 3 restaurants in Brazil to appear on the coveted San Pellegrino 'World's Best' list.

$$$-$$ AK Vila, R Fradique Coutinho 1240, Vila Madalena, T011-3231 4496, www.akvila.com.br. After moving back to her native São Paulo from New York, former film-producer Andrea Kaufmann resolved to open a New York-style deli. The restaurant won numerous awards, including the Folha de São Paulo restaurant-of-the-year, leading Kaufmann to expand to Vila Madalena where her far broader menu includes light on the waistline seafood, petiscos and steaks, as well as sandwiches and bagels from the deli counter.

$$ Goshala, R dos Pinheiros 267, Pinheiros, T011-3063 0367, www.goshala.com.br. Brazilian with and Indian fare – cheese samosas with pupunha taste more like a pastel than the real thing, the curries are moquecas by another name. But there's plenty of choice and variety and the menu is 100% veggie.

$$ Peixeria, R Inacio Pereira da Rocha 112, T011-2859 3963. This rustic-chic fish restaurant with raw brick walls, wood tables, colanders for lampshades and a giant model tarpon suspended from the ceiling draws a fashionable crowd sick of the inflated prices of gourmet São Paulo and seduced by the ultra-fresh fish, seafood petiscos and modest bills.

$$-$ Deli Paris, R Harmonia 484, Vila Madalena, T011-3816 5911, www.deliparis.com.br. This Paulistano homage to a French café serves light and flavourful sweet and savoury crêpes, sickly sweet petit gateaux au chocolat, cheese-heavy quiches, salads and crunchy sandwiches to a busy lunchtime and evening crowd.

$$-$ Genial, R Girassol 374, T011-3812 7442, www.bargenial.com.br. This bar, with a black-and-white mosaic floor and black-tie waiters, is decorated with LP covers by famous traditional musicians such as João do Vale and Luiz Gonzaga. The *chope* is creamy and best accompanied by a *petisco* bar snack, like *caldinho de feijão* (bean broth) or *bolinhos de bacalhau* (codfish balls), both of which are among the best in Vila Madalena. There's a hearty and very popular *feijoada* on Sat and Sun lunch.

South of the centre *p40, map p26*
Liberdade is dotted with Japanese restaurants and has a lively market on Sun with plenty of food stalls. Bela Vista is replete with Italian restaurants, most of them rather poor, with stodgy pasta and gooey risotto. Ibirauera Park has lots of mobile snack bars selling ice cream, sugar cane juice, hot dogs and snacks, and there is a good-value buffet restaurant close to the Museu Afro Brasileiro.

$$$-$$ Famiglia Mancini, R Anhandava, T011-3255 6599, www.famigliamancini. com.br. This pretty little pedestrianized street 10 mins' walk from the Terraço Italia is lined with Italian restaurants and delicatessens, almost all of them in the locally owned **Famiglia Mancini** group. Here, the big dining room with formal waiters and an enormous menu of meats, pastas, risottos, fish and (inevitably for São Paulo) pizzas, is the family's flagship restaurant. Walls are lined with the faces of famous Brazilians who have dined here.

$$ Aska Lámen, R Galvão Buemno 466, Liberadade, T011-3277 9682. One of Liberadade's more traditional Japanese restaurants with a bar overlooking an open kitchen where chefs serve piping ramen noodle dishes to lunchtime diners who are 90% *issei* (Japanese immigrants and their descendants).

$$ Prêt, Museu de Arte Moderna (MAM), Parque Ibirapuera, T011-5574 1250, www. mam.org.br. Closed evenings. The best food in the park: ultra-fresh pre-prepared soups, salads, chicken, fish, meat and vegetarian dishes.

$$ Sushi Yassu, R Tomas Gonzaga 98, T011-3288 2966, www.sushiyassu.com. br. The best of Liberdade's traditional Japanese restaurants with a large menu of sushi/sashimi combinations, teishoku (complete set meals with cooked and raw dishes) and very sweet Brazilianized desserts.

Itaím, Vila Olímpia, Moema and Vila Nova Conceição *p43, map p26*
These areas, south of the centre, have dozens of ultra-trendy restaurants with beautiful people posing in beautiful surroundings. We include only a handful of the best.

$$$ 348 Parrilla Porteña, R Comendador Miguel Calfat, 348, Vila Olímpia, T011-3849 0348, www.restaurante348.com.br. An Argentinian restaurant with the best steak in the country and the choicest cuts available on export from Buenos Aires. The *ojo del bife* cuts like brie and collapses in the mouth like wafered chocolate. The accompanying wines are equally superb, especially the 2002 Cheval dos Andes. Great, unpretentious atmosphere.

$$$ Attimo, R Diogo Jacome, 341, Vila Nova Conceição, T011-5054 9999, www. attimorestaurante.com.br. Super-rich socialite and restaurateur Marcelo Fernandes opened the newest hot spot on the busy São Paulo restaurant scene in late 2012. Star São Paulo chef Jefferson Rueda (formerly of **Pomodori**) heads the kitchen and crafted his menu after months touring the Michelin-starred restaurants of Europe, including **El Celler de Can Roca**.

$$$ Kinoshita, R Jacques Félix 405, Vila Nova Conceição, T011-3849 6940, www. restaurantekinoshita.com.br. Tsuyoshi Murakami offers the best menu of traditional cooked or Kappo cuisine in Brazil, dotted with creative fusion dishes in a **Nobu** vein. His cooking utilizes only the freshest ingredients and includes a sumptuous degustation menu with delights such as tuna marinated in soya, ginger and garlic, served with ponzo sauce and garnished with kaiware (sprouted daikon radish seeds). Murakami trained in the ultra-traditional 100-year-old **Ozushi** restaurant in Tokyo, **Shubu Shubu** in New York and **Kyokata** in Barcelona.

$$$ La Mar, R Tabapuã 1410, Itaim, T011-3073 1213, www.lamarcebicheria.com. **La Mar** brings Peruvian seafood flavours to

São Paulo. Most of the tangy ceviches have been spiced-down for the more sensitive Brazilian palate (though there's a caliente option for those used to chilli and a choice degustation for beginners).

$$$ Parigi, R Amauri 275, Itaim, T011-3167 1575, www.fasano.com.br. One of the premier places to be seen; celebrity couples come here for intimate, public-view Franco-Italian dining. The menu also has classical French dishes such as *coq au vin*. Attractive dining room, beautifully lit, and decked out in lush dark wood.

🎧 Bars, clubs and live music

With no beach, Paulistanos meet for drinks and dancing and the city is prides itself on having great nightlife. There is live music on most nights of the week. Large concert venues, such as the **Pacaembu Stadium**, host the likes of U2 or Ivete Sangalo. Medium-sized venues, such as **Credicard Hall**, are played by acts like Caetano Veloso, Gilberto Gil and Chico Buarque. Smaller venues include **SESCs** (cultural centres with excellent concert halls), and are found in Vila Mariana and Pompéia. They host smaller, classy artists such as Otto, Naná Vasconcelos, João Bosco and Seu Jorge. It is also worth checking out the established smaller live venues in and around Vila Madalena and Itaim, such as **Bourbon St**, **A Marcenaria** and **Grazie a Dio** for samba-funk acts such as Tutti Baê and Funk como le Gusta, designated samba bars like **Ó do Borogodó** (also in Vila Madalena) and venues on the burgeoning alternative music scence, such as the **CB Bar** and **Studio SP** in Barra Funda and Consolação, respectively.

DJs like Marky, and the sadly deceased Suba, made the São Paulo club scene world famous, but gone are the days when Marky was resident DJ at the **Lov.E Club** and the city danced to home-grown sounds in clubs like **Prime**. São Paulo's sound systems and clubs are slicker and swankier than they have ever been, but the music is painfully derivative of New York and Europe.

The city has a bar at every turn – from spit-and-sawdust corner bars serving cold lager beer to an unpretentious blue-collar cord, to smarter *botecos* where penguin-suited waiters whirl around the tables brandishing frothy glasses of draught lager or *chope* (pronounced 'chopee') and self-consciously chic cocktail bars where Paulistano high society flashes its Vartanian jewels and flexes its gym-toned pecs beneath its Osklen. Almost all serve food and many have live music. Beer and snacks are also available at the bar in any *padaria* (bakery).

Barra Funda *p34, map p26*
This dark and edgy neighbourhood northwest of Luz is dotted with dance clubs and venues playing host to a bewildering variety of acts which have little to nothing in common beyond existing beyond the mainstream. It's not safe to walk around here after dark. Take the *metrô* and a cab.
Bar do Alemão, Av Antártica 554, Água Branca, T011-3879 0070, http://bardoalemao.zip.net. This cosy little brick-walled bar and restaurant, on an ugly main road in a semi-residential quarter of Barra Funda, is famous for its live samba. There are samba shows most nights with an especially lively crowd at the weekends. Clara Nunes used to play here and famous samba musicians often appear, including Paulo Cesar Pinheiro and Eduardo Gudin.
Clash Club, R Barra Funda 969, T011-3661 1500, www.clashclub.com.br. Funky and intimate modern club with space for just a few hundred 20-somethings, decorated with raw brick and lit with cellular lights and 3D projections. Music varies hard core techno and hip hop and rare groove. Few Brazilian sounds.
D-Edge, Alameda Olga 170, T011-3667 8334, www.d-edge.com.br. São Paulo's leading temple to electronica is one of the few clubs of this kind to play Brazilian as well as international sounds. However,

those searching for something new will be disappointed by the homages to Ibiza and New York which dominate on most nights. The sound-systems, however, are superb.

SESC Pompeia, R Clélia, 93. Pompéia, T011-3871 7700, www.sescsp.org.br. There's always a great show at this arts and cultural centre in the neighbouring *bairro* to Barra Funda. Some of Brazil's best small acts play at weekends.

The Week, R Guaicurus 324, Barra Funda, T011-3872 9966, www.theweek.com.br. One of the city's biggest gay- and lesbian-dominated dance clubs.

Avenida Paulista and Consolação
p35 and p37, map p36

Until a few years ago the dark streets of Consolação were home to little more than rats, sleazy strip bars, street-walkers and curb-crawlers, but now it harbours a thriving alternative weekend scene with a new club opening virtually every other day.

Astronete, R Augusta 335, Consolação, T011-3151 4568, www.astronete.tumblr.com. One of the area's longest-established clubs drawing a mixed crowd from mock Brit popsters to emo 20-somethings and resolute rockers. The bands and DJs are equally varied – from Mickey Leigh (Joey Ramone's brother) to Pernambuco rap rocker China.

Beco 203, R Augusta 609, Consolação, T011-2339 0351, www.beco203.com.br. Cutting edge alternative rockers from Brazil and the world over play here. Past acts have included the newly reformed Television, British indie Shoegazers Foals, Pata de Elefante and alternative scene DJs like Gabriel Machuca.

Caos, R Augusta 584, Consolação, T011-2365 1260. One of the area's newer and most popular bars with an astonishing variety of music spun by local DJs from Speed Caravan and Serbian gypsy rock to Algerian Rai disco and vintage soul.

Clube Royal, R Consolação 222, T011-3129 9804, www.royalclub.com.br. One of the most fashionable funk and rare groove clubs

on the young, wealthy and need-to-be-seen São Paulo circuit is decorated like a New York dive bar in Brazilian tropical colours. Don't expect to hear any Brazilian music.

Inferno, R Augusta 501, Consolação, T011-3120 4140. www.inferno.com.br. Pounding rock, thrashing metal and the occasional svelte samba-funk act play to a packed crowd at this leopard-skin lined sweaty club.

Kabul, R Pedro Taques 124, Consolação, T011-2503 2810, www.kabul.com.br. Live music ranging from Brazilian jazz to samba rock, and alternative acts. DJs play between and after shows. Lively and eclectic crowd.

Mono, R Augusta 480, T011-2371 0067. A good looking 20- and 30-something crowd gather here to dance to international drum'n'bass and soul (Thu), house (Fri) and rock and disco (Sat). The decor is very typical of Consolação: low-lighting, off-the-wall retro movie projections, quirky stills from Scarface, pick-up trucks, huge 1950s fridges, etc.

Outs Club, R Augusta 486, T011-6867 6050, www.clubeouts.com. One of the bastions of the alternative, rock and hard rock scene with a mix of DJs playing everything from UK indie to heavy Brazilian metal bands.

Studio SP, R Augusta 591, T011-3129 7040, www.studiosp.org. A show hall on the neighbourhood's main thoroughfare. Turning up for the support act (usually before 2200) means getting in for free to see the main show.

Vegas Club, R Augusta 765, T011-3231 3705, www.vegasclub.com.br. Tue-Sat. International and local DJs spin a predictable menu of techno, psi-trance and house to a mixed gay and straight crowd dancing on 2 sweaty floors.

Volt, R Haddock Lobo 40, Consolação, T011-2936 4041, www.barvolt.com.br. Just across Av Paulista from Consolação, a hip creative industry crowd sip fruit *batidas* to Brazilian drum'n'bass and Chicago house in this 400-sq-m space. It's lit with luminescent pink and green strip lights and decorated with a mirror wall, vertical fern garden and Eames wooden chairs and is a favourite pre- and post-club stop.

Jardins *p38, map p36*

Bar Balcão, R Doutor Melo Alves 150, T011-3063 6091. After-work meeting place, very popular with young professionals and media types who gather on either side of the long low wooden bar, which winds its way around the room like a giant snake.
Barretto, Fasano Hotel (see Where to stay, page 48). A rather conservative atmosphere with heavy dark wood, mirrors and cool live bossa jazz. The crowd is mostly the Cuban cigar type with a sprinkling of the tanned and toned, in figure-enhancing designer labels.
Casa de Francisca, R José Maria Lisboa 190 at Brigadeiro Luís Antônio, T011-3493 5717, www.casadefrancisca.art.br. This intimate, live music restaurant-bar plays host to the refined end of the musical spectrum with acts such as virtuoso guitarist and composer Chico Saraiva, multi-instrumentalist Arthur de Faria or pianist Paulo Braga. The best tables to book are those on the upper deck.
Dry Bar, R Padre João Manuel 700, T011-3729 6653, www.drybar.com.br. This low-lit, dark lounge bar and late-night club, has been a favourite with Jardins' rich and very fashionable youngish and single for years now, who throng here in the late evening to drink from a menu of more than a dozen dry martinis. The club was completely re-modelled in 2012.
Finnegan's Pub, R Cristiano Viana 358, Pinheiros, T011-3062 3232, www.finnegan.com.br. One of São Paulo's Irish bars. This one is actually run and owned by an Irishman and is very popular with expats.
Skye, the rooftop bar at **Unique Hotel** (see Where to stay, page 49). Another fashionable spot with a definite door policy.

Vila Madalena and Pinheiros *p39, map p26*

Vila Madalena and adjacent Pinheiros lie just northeast of Jardins. A taxi from Jardins is about US$7.50; there is also a *metrô* station, but this closes by the time the bars get going. These suburbs are the favourite haunts of São Paulo 20-somethings, more hippy chic than Itaim, less stuffy than Jardins. This is the best part of town for live Brazilian music and uniquely Brazilian close dances such as *forró*, as opposed to international club sounds. It can feel grungy and informal but is buzzing. The liveliest streets are Aspicuelta and Girassol.
A Marcenaria, R Fradique Coutinho 1378, T011-3032 9006, www.amarcenaria.com.br. This is the Vila Madalena bar of choice for the young, single lovers of Brazilian rock who gather here from 2130; the dance floor fills up at around 2300.
Bambu, R Purpurina 272, Vila Madalena, T011-3031 2331, www.bambubrasilbar.com.br. A kind of backland desert jig called *forró* has everyone up and dancing in this slice of mock-Bahia, with live northeastern accordion and *zabumba* drum bands in the front room and a hippy middle-class student crowd downing industrial strength caipirinhas out the back.
Canto da Ema, Av Brigadeiro Faria Lima 364, T011-3813 4708, www.cantodaema.com.br. Very popular *forró* club with great live bands from the northeast.
Grazie a Dio, R Girassol 67, T011-3031 6568, www.grazieadio.com.br. The best bar in Vila Madalena to hear live music. There's a different (but always quality) band every night with acts ranging from Banda Gloria, Clube do Balanco and Japanese-Brazilian samba-funk band Sambasonics. Great for dancing. Always packed.
Ó do Borogodó, R Horácio Lane 21, Vila Madalena, T011-3814 4087. It can be hard to track down this intimate club opposite the cemetery. It's in an unmarked house next to a hairdressers on the edge of Vila Madalena. The tiny dance hall is always

packed with people between Wed and Sat. On Wed there's classic samba canção from retired cleaner Dona Inah who sings material from the likes of Cartola and Ataulfo Alves; and on other nights there's a varied programme of *choro*, and MPB from some of the best samba players in São Paulo.

Posto 6, R Aspicuelta 644, Vila Madalena, T011-3812 7831. An imitation Rio de Janeiro *boteco* with attractive crowds and backdrop of bossa nova and MPB. Busy from 2100.

Sub Astor, R Delfina 163, Vila Madalena, T011-3815 1364, www.subastor.com.br. This velvety mood-lit lounge bar looks like a film set from a David Lynch movie and is filled with mols, vamps and playboys from the upper echelons of São Paulo society. The cocktails are superb.

Itaím, Vila Olímpia and Moema *p43, map p26*

This area, just south of Ibirapuera and north of the new centre, is about US$12.50 by taxi from Jardins and US$15 from the centre, but well worth the expense of getting here. It is packed with street-corner bars, which are great for a browse. The bars here, although informal, have a style of their own, with lively and varied crowds and decent service. The busiest streets for a bar wander are: R Atilio Inocenti, near the junction of Av Juscelino Kubitschek and Av Brigadeiro Faria Lima; Av Hélio Pellegrino; and R Araguari, which runs behind it.

Bourbon Street Music Club, R dos Chanés 127, Moema, T011-5095 6100, www. bournbonstreet.com.br. Great little club with acts like funkster Tutti Bae, Funk Como Le Gusta, Max de Castro and Wilson Simoninha and international acts like BB King.

Disco, R Professor Atílio Inocennti 160, Itaim, T011-3078 0404, www.clubdisco. com.br. One of the city's plushest high-society discos and a favourite with leading socialites and models, especially during Fashion Week. The decor is by Isay Weinfeld

who designed the **Fasano**, and the music standard Eurotrash and US club sounds.

Na Mata Café, R da Mata 70, Itaim, T011-3079 0300, www.namata.com. br. Popular flirting and pick-up spot for 20- and 30-somethings who gyrate in the dark dance room to a variety of Brazilian and European dance tunes and select live bands. Decent comfort food and snacks.

Provocateur, R Jerônimo Da Veiga 163, Itaim Bibi, T011-2339 2597, www. provocateurclubsp.com.br. São Paulo's love affair with New York nightlife continues with the opening of the Latin American branch of the modish Manhattan nightclub.

😃 Entertainment

São Paulo *p18, maps p26, p28 and p36*

For listings of concerts, theatre, museums, galleries and cinemas visit www.guiasp.com. br, or check out the *Guia da Folha* section of *Folha de São Paulo*, and the *Veja São Paulo* section of the weekly news magazine *Veja*.

Cinema

Entrance is usually half price on Wed; normal seat price is US$10. Most shopping centres have multiplexes showing the latest blockbuster releases. These are usually in their original language with Portuguese subtitles (*legendas*). Where they are not, they are marked 'DUB' (*dublado*).

There are arts cinemas at the **SESC**s (notably at the **Cine Sesco**, R Augusta 2075, Jardins, T011-3087 0500, www.cinesescsp. org.br, and at **Pompeia** and **Vila Mariana**, www.sescsp.org.br); and at the **Centro Cultural Banco do Brasil** (see page 30).

Other arts cinemas are at **Belas Artes** (R da Consolação 2423, T011-3258 4092, www.confrariadecinema.com.br); **Espaço Unibanco** (R Augusta 1470/1475, www. unibancocinemas.com.br); **Museu da Imagem e do Som** (Av Europa 258, T011-2117 4777, www.mis-sp.org.br); **Itaú Cultural** (www.itaucultural.org.br); and

Centro Cultural São Paulo (www.centro cultural.sp.gov.br), see below.

Classical music, ballet and theatre
In addition to those listed below, there are several other 1st-class theatres: **Aliança Francesa**, R Gen Jardim 182, Vila Buarque, T011-3259 0086; **Itália**, Av Ipiranga 344, T011-3257 9092; **Paiol**, R Amaral Gurgel 164, Santa Cecília, T011-3221 2462; free concerts at **Teatro Popular do Sesi**, Av Paulista 1313, T011-3284 9787, Mon-Sat 1200, under MASP.

Centro Cultural São Paulo, R Vergueiro 1000, T011-3397 4002, www.centrocultural. sp.gov.br. A 50,000-sq-m arts centre with concert halls, where there are regular classical music and ballet recitals, with an orchestral performance most Sun afternoons and a concerto most lunchtimes (in the Sala Adoniran Barbosa), a library with work desks, theatres and exhibition spaces.

Sala São Paulo (see page 33). This magnificent neo-gothic hall with near perfect acoustics is the city's premier classical music venue and is home to Brazil's best orchestra, the Orquestra Sinfônica do Estado de São Paulo (www.osesp.art.br). The OSESP has been cited as one of 3 up-and-coming ensembles in the ranks of the world's greatest orchestras by the English magazine *Gramophone*. They have a busy schedule of performances (details available on their website) with concerts usually on Thu, Fri and Sat.

Teatro Municipal Opera House (see page 32). Used by visiting theatrical and operatic groups, as well as the City Ballet Company and the Municipal Symphony Orchestra, who give regular performances. Fully refurbished in 2012.

✺ Festivals

São Paulo *p18, maps p26, p28 and p36*
Throughout the year there are countless anniversaries, religious feasts, fairs and exhibitions. To see what's on, check the local press or the monthly tourist magazines. Fashion Week is held in the Bienal Centre (Bienal do Ibirapuera) in Ibirapuera Park, T011-5576 7600.

25 Jan Foundation of the city.

Feb Carnaval. *Escolas de samba* parade in the Anhembi Sambódromo. During Carnaval most museums and attractions are closed.

Jun Festas Juninas and the Festa de São Vito, the patron saint of the Italian immigrants.

Sep Festa da Primavera.

Nov Formula One Grand Prix at Interlagos.

Dec Christmas and New Year festivities.

⊙ Shopping

São Paulo *p18, maps p26, p28 and p36*
São Paulo isn't the best place to shop for souvenirs, but it remains Latin America's fashion and accessory capital and the best location in the southern hemisphere for quality fashion and jewellery.

Books and music
Livrarias Saraiva and Laselva are found in various shopping malls and at airports, they sell books in English. FNAC, Av Paulista 901 (at Metrô Paraíso) and Praça Omaguás 34, Pinheiros (Metrô Pinheiros), www.fnac.com. br, has a huge choice of DVDs, CDs, books in Portuguese (and English), magazines and newspapers.

Fashion boutiques
São Paulo is one of the newest hot spots on the global fashion circuit and is by far the most influential and diverse fashion city in South America. The designers based here have collections as chic as any in Europe or North America. Best buys include smart casual day wear, bikinis, shoes, jeans and leather jackets. Havaiana flip flops, made famous by Gisele Bundchen and Fernanda Tavares, are around 60% of the price of

The Brazilian Grand Prix

Motor racing has had a long and distinguished history in Brazil and the first race day at Interlagos took place on 12 May 1940. The first Brazilian Grand Prix was held here in 1972 and Emerson Fittipaldi drove to victory in front of a home crowd in 1973 and 1974. The following year another Brazilian, José Carlos Pace (after whom the track is officially named Autódromo José Carlos Pace), was first to cross the chequered flags.

During the 1980s the Grand Prix race was held at the Jacarepaguá racetrack in Rio where the outspoken Nelson Piquet won twice in 1983 and 1986 with some of the fastest lap times seen on this track.

The race returned to the improved Interlagos track during the 1990s, and the legendary Aryton Senna won here in 1991 and 1993. After his tragic death in 1994, as a result of mechanical failure, Brazilian viewing figures for motor racing fell drastically but picked up with the success of Rubens Barrichello and Felipe Massa in the new millennium.

The Brazilian Grand Prix is usually the last race of the season, held in October or November. The race consists of 72 laps with a total distance of 309.024 km. Approximately 55,000 people attend, in addition to millions watching around the world. The training session takes place on Friday morning; the time trial on Saturday morning and the race itself on Sunday afternoon with warm-ups and the drivers' parade in the morning.

Tickets can be bought from the racetrack during the whole week or by contacting ABN Amro Bank on T011-5507 500 from abroad and T0800-170200 inside Brazil. Minimum ticket price is US$100 rising to US$350 depending on the viewing sector. Sectors A and G are uncovered and the cheapest, whilst sector D is covered, provides a better view and is more expensive. Tickets for the training sessions are cheaper and can be bought from 0700 on the day from the box office at the circuit. VIP hospitality is readily available but at a high price.

There is no parking for private vehicles at the racetrack, but park-and-ride facilities (US$5) are available on Saturday from Shopping SP Market, Avenida das Nações Unidas 22540, and on Sunday from Hipermercado, Avenida das Nações Unidas 4403 and Shopping Interlagos, Avenida Interlagos 2255. There are also buses (Saturday-Sunday) from Praça da República, between Rua do Arouche and Rua Marquês de Itu (No 295), from Praça Com Lineu Gomes at Congonhas airport and from Rua dos Jequitibás in front of the Jabaquara bus station (No 189). All buses have coloured stickers to indicate which drop-off point they serve. Further information about the Grand Prix in English can be obtained from www.gpbrasil.com, www.gpbrasil.com.br or www.formula1.com. **Matueté** (see page 65) can organize packages to the Grand Prix, with all transport, accommodation and pick-up from the airport.

Europe. The best areas for fashion shopping are Jardins (around R Oscar Freire) and the **Iguatemi Shopping Centre** (Av Faria Lima), while the city's most exclusive shopping emporium is **Shopping JK** (see page 64). In late 2013 look out for the first **Issa** boutique in Brazil, opened by designer Daniella Helayel who made her name in London, becoming a favourite designer for Catherine Duchess of Cambridge.
Adriana Barra, Alameda Franca 1243, T011-2925 2300, www.adrianabarra.com.br.

Her showroom is in a converted residential house whose façade is entirely covered with vines, bromeliads and ferns. Adriana is best known for her long dresses and bell-sleeved tunics, made of silk and jersey and printed with designs which take classic belle époque French floral and abstract motifs and reinterpret them in 1970s tropicalia-laced colours and patterns. She now sells homeware, with everything from sofas and scatter cushions to bedspreads, amphorae and notebooks.

Adriana Degreas, R Dr Melo Alves 734, Jardins, T011-3064 4300, www.adriana degreas.com.br. Adriana opened her flagship store in Jardins with a zesty collection premiered at Claro Rio Summer Fashion Show. She now sells at Barneys and Bloomingdales in New York and in Selfridges in London.

Alexandre Herchcovitz, R Melo Alves 561, T011-4306 6457, www.herchcovitch.uol. com.br, Perhaps the most famous young Brazilian designer, using brightly coloured materials to create avant garde designs influenced by European trends but with their own decidedly tropical bent.

Carina Duek, R Oscar Freire 736, T011-2359 5972, www.carinaduek.com.br. Another rising young star opened this boutique in 2009, designed by **Fasano** architect Isay Weinfeld. Her simple, figure-hugging light summer dresses and miniskirts are favourites with 20-something Paulistana socialites.

Carlos Miele, R Bela Cintra 2231 and **Shopping Cidade Jardim**, Consolação, T011-3062 6144, www.carlosmiele.com. br. Modern Brazil's biggest international brand with collections sold in more than 30 countries and his own brand- name shops in New York and Paris. His bright, slick and sexy prêt-à-porter designs have been used in TV shows from Ugly Betty to Gossip Girl. In Brazil, Carlos Miele is best known for **M.Officer** (branches in major malls), a brand celebrated for jeans and casual wear.

Fause Haten, Alameda Lorena 1731, Jardins, T011-3081 8685, www.fausehaten. com.br. One of Brazil's most internationally renowned designers who works in plastic, lace, leather, mohair and denim with laminate appliqués, selling through, amongst others, **Giorgio Beverly Hills**.

Forum, R Oscar Freire 916, Jardins, T011-3085 6269, www.forum.com.br. A huge white space attended by beautiful shop assistants helping impossibly thin 20-something Brazilians squeeze into tight, but beautifully cut, jeans and other fashion items.

Iodice, R Oscar Freire 940, T011-3085 9310, and **Shopping Iguatemi**, T011-3813 2622, www.iodice.com.br. Sophisticated and innovative knitwear designs sold abroad in boutiques like **Barney's NYC**.

Lenny, Shopping Iguatemi, T011-3032 2663, R Sarandi 98, T011-3798 2044, and R Escobar Ortiz 480, Vila Nova Conceicao, T011-3846 6594, www.lenny.com.br. Rio de Janeiro's premier swimwear designer and Brazil's current favourite.

Mario Queiroz, R Alameda Franca 1166, T011-3062 3982, www.marioqueiroz.com. br. Casual and elegant clothes with a strong gay element, for 20-something men.

Osklen, R Oscar Freire, 645, T011-3083 7977, www.osklen.com. Brazil's answer to Ralph Lauren, with stylish but casual beach and boardwalk wear for men.

Ricardo Almeida, Bela Cintra 2093, T011-3887 4114, and **Shopping JK**. One of the few Brazilian designers who styles for men. His clothes are a range of dark suits, slick leather jackets and finely cut and tailored jeans.

Ronaldo Fraga, R Aspicuelta 259, Vila Madalena, T011-3816 2181, www.ronaldo fraga.com. Fraga's adventurous collection combines discipline with daring, retaining a unified style across the sexes yet always surprising and delighting with its off-the-wall creativity.

UMA, R Girassol 273, T011-3813 5559, www.uma.com.br. Raquel Davidowicz offers rails of sleek contemporary cuts set against low-lit, cool white walls with a Japanese-inspired monochrome minimalism mixed with colourful Brazilian vibrancy.

Victor Hugo, R Oscar Freire 816, T011-3082 1303, www.victorhugo.com.br. Brazil's most fashionable handbag designer.

Zoomp, R Oscar Freire 995, T011-3064 1556, **Shopping Iguatemi**, T011-3032 5372, www.zoomp.com.br. **Zoomp** has been famous for its figure-hugging jeans for nearly 3 decades and has grown to become a nationwide and now international brand.

Bargain fashion If the upper crust shop and sip coffee in Jardins, the rest of the city buys its wares on the other side of the old city centre in Bom Retiro (Metrô Mal Deodoro, CPTM Julio Prestes/Luz). At first sight the neighbourhood is relentlessly urban: ugly concrete with rows of makeshift houses converted into hundreds of shops selling a bewildering array of clothing. Much of it is trash, and during the week wholesale stores may specify a minimum number of items per buyer. But a few hours browsing will yield clothing bargains to rival those in Bangkok. Many of the outfitters manufacture for the best mid-range labels in São Paulo, including those in **Shopping Ibirapuera** (see Shopping malls, below). The best shopping is on and around R José Paulino – a street with more than 350 shops. The best day to come is Sat from 0800, when most items are sold individually.

Shopping 25 de Março, R 25 de Março, www.25demarco.com.br, Metrô São Bento, in the city centre offers a similarly large range of costume jewellery, toys and small decorative items (best on Sat 0800-1430).

The neighbourhood of **Brás** stocks lower quality cheaper items. For more information see www.omelhordobomretiro.com.br.

Handicrafts

São Paulo has no handicrafts tradition but some items from the rest of Brazil can be bought at Parque Tte Siqueira Campos/Trianon on Sun 0900-1700.

Casa dos Amazonas, Al dos Jurupis 460, Moema, www.arteindigena.com.br. Huge variety of Brazilian indigenous arts and crafts from all over the country.

Galeria Arte Brasileira, Av Lorena 2163, T011-3062 9452, www.galeriaartebrasileira.com.br. Folk art from the northeast, including the famous clay figurines from Caruaru, Ceará lace, Amazonian hammocks, carved wooden items from all over the country and indigenous Brazilian bead and wicker art.

Sutaco, R Boa Vista 170, Edif Cidade I, 3rd floor, Centro, T011-3241 7333. Handicrafts shop selling and promoting items from the state of São Paulo.

Jewellery

Antonio Bernardo, R Bela Cintra 2063, Jardins, T011-3083 5622, www.antonio bernardo.com.br. Bernardo is as understated as **Vartanian** is bling, and offers elegant, contemporary gold and platinum designs and exquisite stones. The designer has branches all over the city and in locations throughout Brazil.

H Stern, www.hstern.com.br, with shops all over the city including: R Augusta 2340; R Oscar Freire 652; at **Iguatemi**, **Ibirapuera**, **Morumbi**, **Paulista** and other shopping centres; at large hotels; and at the international airport. Brazil's biggest jewellers, represented in 18 countries. In Brazil they have designs based on Brazilian themes, including Amazonian bead art and Orixa mythology.

Vartanian, NK, R Bela Cintra 2175, Jardins, and **Shopping JK**, T011-3061 5738, www.jackvartanian.com. Jack Vartanian creates fashion jewellery with huge Brazilian emeralds and diamonds set in simple gold and platinum – much beloved of Hollywood red-carpet walkers including Zoe Saldana, Cameron Diaz and Demi Moore. His low-lit Jardins shop showcases jewellery only available only in Brazil.

Markets

Ceasa Flower Market, Av Doutor Gastão Vidigal 1946, Jaguaré. Tue and Fri 0700-1200. Should not be missed.

MASP Antiques Market, takes place below the museum. Sun 1000-1700. Some 50 stalls selling everything from vintage gramophones to ceramics, ornaments and old vinyl.

Mercado Municipal, R da Cantareira 306, Centro, T011-3326 3401, www.mercado municipal.com.br. Metrô São Bento. This newly renovated art deco market was built at the height of the coffee boom and is illuminated by beautiful stained-glass panels by Conrado Sorgenicht Filho showing workers tilling the soil. It's worth coming here just to browse aisles bursting with produce: *açai* from the Amazon, hunks of *bacalhau* from the North Sea, mozzarella from Minas, sides of beef from the Pantanal and 1000 other foodstuffs. The upper gallery has half a dozen restaurants offering dishes of the day and a vantage point over the frenetic buying and selling below.

Oriental Fair, Praça de Liberdade. Sun 1000-1900. Good for Japanese snacks, plants and some handicrafts, very picturesque, with remedies on sale, tightrope walking, gypsy fortune tellers, etc.

Praça Benedito Calixto, Pinheiros, www. pracabeneditocalixto.com.br. Metrô Pinheiros. The best bric-a-brac market in São Paulo takes place here Sat 0900-1900, with live *choro* and samba 1430-1830. There are many stylish shops, restaurants and cafés around the square.

Av Lorena, which is one of the upmarket shopping streets off R Augusta in Jardins, has an open-air market on Sun selling fruits and juices. There is a flea market on Sun in **Praça Don Orione** (main square of the Bixiga district).

There is also a Sunday market in the **Praça da República** in the city centre (see page 32).

Shopping malls and department stores

For more information on shopping malls, see www.shoppingsdesaopaulo.com.br.

Shopping Cidade Jardim, Av Magalhães de Castro 12000, T011-3552 1000, www. cidadejardimshopping.com.br. CPTM Hebraica-Rebouças (and then 5-10 mins by taxi). Brazilian names like **Carlos Miele** and **Osklen**, whose casual beach and adventure clothes look like Ralph Lauren gone tropical and are aimed at a similar yacht-and-boardwalk crowd.

Shopping Ibirapuera, Av Ibirapuera 3103, www.ibirapuera.com.br, Metrô Ana Rosa and bus 695V (Terminal Capelinha). A broad selection of mid-range Brazilian labels and general shops including toy and book shops.

Shopping Iguatemi, Av Brigadeiro Faria Lima 2232, www.iguatemisaopaulo.com. br. A top-end shopping mall just south of Jardins with a healthy representation of most of Brazil's foremost labels.

Shopping JK Iguatemi, Av Presidente Juscelino Kubitschek 2041, Vila Olimpia, T011-3152 6800, www.jkiguatemi.com.br. The fashion, jewellery and lifestyle shopping centre of choice for São Paulo's high society, wannabes and window shoppers. With many of Brazil's choicest labels from Daslu to Carlos Miele and international names like Burberry, Calvin Klein, Diesel and Chanel. Also houses one of the city's best cinemas and a huge food court.

⊘ What to do

São Paulo *p18, maps p26, p28 and p36*

Football

The most popular local teams are Corinthians, Palmeiras and São Paulo who generally play in the Morumbi and Pacaembu stadiums.

Tour operators

São Paulo has several large agencies offering tours around the country.

Ambiental Viagens e Expedições, www.ambiental.tur.br. Good for trips to less well-known places throughout the country, such as Jalapão. English/Spanish spoken, helpful.

Matueté, R Tapinás 22, Itaim, T011-3071 4515, www.matuete.com. Luxury breaks throughout Brazil and city tours, including personal shopping. Ask for Camilla. English spoken.

SPin Brazil Tours, T011-5904 2269/T011-9185 2623 (mob), www.spintours.com.br. Tailor-made services and private tours of São Paulo city and state with options on destinations further afield. These include bilingual 3- to 4-hr tours of the city of São Paulo (including key sights like the Football Museum, Edif Italia and MASP), tailor-made bilingual tours tailored to visitor interest, and coordinated visits to football matches and the Brazilian Grand Prix. Expect to pay from US$50 per hr for a simple city tour and around US$75 per hr for special interest tours. SPin can arrange accommodation for a surcharge and offer a driver/guide service for business trips. Comfortable cars. Excellent organization.

⊖ Transport

São Paulo p18, maps p26, p28 and p36

Air

See also Getting to São Paulo, page 6.

Guarulhos International Airport (Cumbica), www.aeroportoguarulhos.net, operates services to all parts of the world and much of Brazil. The cheapest internal flights are with **TAM**, www.tam.com.br, **GOL**, www.voegol.com.br, **Azul**, www.voeazul.com.br (which also flies from Campinas, page 19), and **Avianca**, www.avianca.com.br. If you have a flight connection to Congonhas, your airline will provide a courtesy bus. The best way to reach the city/airport is on the fast, a/c **Airport Bus Service** (www.airportbusservice.com.br) leaving from outside international Arrivals (and with a ticket office at this location). It has routes as follows: to the Tiete bus terminal (US$18.50, 40 mins); Praça da República (US$17.50, 1 hr); Av Paulista (US$17.50, 1 hr 15 mins); Itaim Bibi (US$17.50, 1 hr 20 mins); Av Luís Carlos Berrini (US$17.50, 1 hr 30 mins); Aeroporto Congonhas (US$17.50, 1 hr 10 mins). Most buses leave at least once an hour 0530-2400 and every 90 mins thereafter (though there are fewer services to Berrini and Itaim). Taxi fares from the city to the airport are US$60-75. There are plans to open a new fast road (with exclusive bus lanes) between the airport and Tucuruvi (on the Linha 1-Azul *metrô* line); this road is not expected to open before 2015. This means that rush-hour traffic can easily turn this 30-min journey into an hour or even longer. Be sure to allow plenty of time for transit and to arrive with plenty of time for checking in as long queues form for immigration and customs: passenger numbers have doubled at Cumbica over the past decade, airport upgrade works are late and insufficient and the airport is often overcrowded.

Congonhas Domestic Airport is used for flights within Brazil, including the shuttle flight to Santos Dumont airport in **Rio de Janeiro** (US$100-150 single, depending on availability). The shuttle services operate every 30 mins throughout the day 0630-2230. Sit on the left-hand side for views to Rio de Janeiro, the other side coming back; book flights in advance. To get to Congonhas Airport, take a bus or *metrô*/bus (see www.sptrans.com.br) or a taxi (roughly US$20 from the centre, Vila Madalena or Jardins).

Bus

See www.buscaonibus.com.br or www.passagem-em-domicilio.com.br for information on the latest services and prices. Both sites give times and routes and redirect to the bus company website, through which it is possible to buy tickets. There are 4 bus terminals: **Tietê, Barra Funda, Bresser** and **Jabaquara**. All are connected to the *metrô* system.

Rodoviária Tietê This is the main bus station and has a convenient *metrô* station. Unfortunately the only way to the platforms is by stairs which makes it very difficult for people with heavy luggage and almost impossible for those in a wheelchair. Tietê handles buses to the interior of São Paulo state, to all state capitals and international destinations. To **Rio**, 6 hrs, every 30 mins, US$35, special section for this route in the *rodoviária*, request the coastal route via Santos (*via litoral*) unless you wish to go the direct route. To **Florianópolis**, 11 hrs, US$110 (*leito* US$95). To **Porto Alegre**, 18 hrs, US$90. To **Curitiba**, 6 hrs, US$35. To **Salvador**, 30 hrs, US$150. To **Recife**, 40 hrs, US$180. To **Campo Grande**, 14 hrs, US$180. To **Cuiabá**, 24 hrs, US$95. To **Porto Velho**, 60 hrs (or more), US$140. To **Brasília**, 16 hrs, US$82.50 (*executivo* US$90). To **Foz do Iguaçu**, 16 hrs, US$50, To **Paraty**, 6 hrs, US$25. To **São Sebastião**, 4 hrs, US$25 (ask for 'via Bertioga' if you want to go by the coast road, a beautiful journey but few buses take this route as it is longer).

International connections Buses to Uruguay, Argentina and Paraguay.

Barra Funda (Metrô Barra Funda), to cities in southern **São Paulo state** and many destinations in Paraná, including **Foz do Iguaçu** (check for special prices on buses to **Ciudad del Este**, which can be cheaper than buses to Foz). Buses to **Cananéia** daily at 0900 and 1430, 4 hrs. Alternatively go via **Registro** (buses hourly), from where there are 7 buses daily to Cananéia and regular connections to **Curitiba**.

Bresser (Metrô Bresser), for **Cometa** (T011-6967 7255) or **Transul** (T011-6693 8061) serving destinations in Minas Gerais. **Belo Horizonte**, 8 hrs, US$45. See www. passagem-em-domicilio.com.br for more information including bus times and the latest prices.

Jabaquara (at the southern end of the *metrô* line), is used by buses to **Santos**, US$10.50, every 15 mins, taking about 50 mins, last bus at 0100. Also serves destinations on the southern coast of São Paulo state.

Car hire
The major names all serve São Paulo and have offices at the airports.

CPTM (urban light railway) → *See map, page 20.*
Ticket prices on the CPTM are the same as the *metrô* (see below and box, opposite).
Linha 7 Rubi (ruby) runs from Jundiaí, a satellite commuter town, to the Estação da Luz via Barra Funda and the Palmeiras football stadium.
Linha 8 Diamante (diamond) runs from Amador Bueno to the Estação Júlio Prestes railway station in Luz, near the Pinacoteca and next to the Estação da Luz via Osasco.
Linha 9 Esmeralda (emerald) runs between the suburb of Osasco and the suburb of Grajaú in the far south. This is the a useful line for tourists as it runs along the Pinheiros river, stopping at Pinheiros (where there will be an interchange for the Metrô Linha Amarela from late 2013), the Cidade Universitária (for Butantã), Hebraica-Rebouças (for shopping Eldorado and the Azul bus to Campinas airport, see page 19), Cidade Jardim (for Shopping Cidade Jardim, see page 64), Vila Olímpia (close to one of the nightlife centres) and Berrini (in the new business district).
Linha 10 Turquesa (turquoise) runs from Rio Grande da Serra in the Serra do Mar mountains (from where there are onward trains to Paranapiacaba, see page 47) to the Estação da Luz.
Linha 11 Coral (coral) runs from the Estudantes suburb in the far east to the Estação Julio Prestes via Mogi das Cruzes, and the Corinthians stadium at Itaquera where one of the key 2014 FIFA World Cup™ stadia lies and where there is an interchange for the Metrô Linha 3 Vermelha. Expect this train service to be very busy.

O Bilhete Único

This electronic ticket is similar to a London Oyster card – integrating bus, *metrô* and light railway in a single, rechargeable plastic swipe card. US$2 serves for one *metrô* or CPTM journey and three bus journeys within the space of three hours. Swipe cards can be bought at *metrô* stations. The initial minimum charge is US$10.

Linha 12 Safira (sapphire) runs from Calmon Viana suburb in the east to Brás where there is an interchange for the Metrô Linha 3 Vermelha.

Metrô → *See map, p20*
Directions are indicated by the name of the terminus station. Network maps are displayed only in the upper concourses of the *metrô* stations; there are none on the platforms. Many of the maps on the internet are confusing as they incorporate the CPTM overground train routes, also with colour codes. Journeys can get extremely crowded at peak times (0700-1000, 1630-1900). Services are also plagued by unannounced and unexplained stops and cancellations. Fares are at a flat rate of US$1.50. The bilhete unico swipe card (which is similar to London's Oyster card) allows you to travel for multiple journeys by topping-up the card and can be used on the CPTM, minibus and bus). See also box, above.
Linha 1 Azul (blue) runs from Tucuruvi in the north to the Rodoviária Jabaraquara in the south and passing through Luz, the centre and Liberdade.
Linha 2 Verde (green) runs from Vila Madalena to Vila Prudente, via Consolação, Av Paulista and the MASP art gallery.
Linha 3 Vermelha (red) runs from the Palmeiras football stadium in Barra Funda to the Corinthians football stadium in Itaquera, via the city centre.
Linha 4 Amarela (yellow) will run between between Morumbi football stadium and Luz, via USP University at Butantã, Oscar Freire in Jardins, Faria Lima and Av Paulista. At present not all the

stations are open (including Oscar Freire) and the line only extends west as far as Butantã but the line is expected to be completed before the 2014 FIFA World Cup™ begins.
Linha 5 Lilás (lilac) running in São Paulo's far southwest, between Capão Redondo *favela* and Adolfo Pinheiro. An extension to Chacara Klabin on the 2 Verde line via Estação Eucaliptus (for Moema and Shopping Ibirapuera) is expected to open between 2014 and 2016.

Taxi
Taxis display cards of actual tariffs in the window (starting price US$1.80). There are ordinary taxis, which are hailed on the street, or at taxi stations such as Praça da República, radio taxis and deluxe taxis. For Radio Taxis, which are more expensive but involve fewer hassles, try: **Central Radio Táxi**, T011-6914 6630; **São Paulo Rádio Táxi**, T011-5583 2000; **Fácil**, T011-6258 5947; or **Aero Táxi**, T011-6461 4090. Alternatively, look in the phone book; calls are not accepted from public phones.

Train
From **Estação da Luz** and **Estação Júlio Prestes** (Metrô Luz).

❶ Directory

São Paulo *p18, maps p26, p28 and p36*
Banks Banking hours are generally 1000-1600, although times differ for foreign exchange. For ATMS, the best bank to use is Bradesco, www.bradesco.com.br, or HSBC,

www.hsbc.com.br, which have branches on every other street corner and ATMs in the airport and all the major shopping malls. Be wary when using ATMs and never use street machines after dark. Most ATMs do not function between 2200 and 0600. **Banco do Brasil** will change cash and TCs and will advance cash against Visa. All transactions are done in the foreign exchange department of any main branch (eg Av São João 32, Centro), but queues are long and commission very high.

Immigration Federal Police, R Hugo D'Antola 95, Lapa de Baixo, T011-3538 5000, www.dpf.gov.br. For visa extensions; allow all day and expect little English (1000-1600). **Internet** Look for any LAN house sign. **Language courses** The official Universidade de São Paulo (USP) is situated in the Cidade Universitária (buses from main bus station), beyond Pinheiros. They have courses available to foreigners, including a popular Portuguese course. Registry is through the **Comissão de Cooperação Internacional**, R do Anfiteatro 181, Bloco das Colméias 05508, Cidade Universitária, São Paulo. Other universities include the **Pontifical Catholic University** (PUC), and the **Mackenzie University**. Both these are more central than the USP, Mackenzie in Higienopolis, just west of the centre, and PUC in Perdizes. Take a taxi to either. Both have notice boards where you can leave a request for Portuguese teachers or language exchange, which is easy to arrange for free. Any of the *gringo* pubs are good places to organize similar exchanges. **Medical services** Hospital das Clínicas, Av Dr Enéias de Carvalho Aguiar 255, Jardins, T011-3069 6000. **Hospital Samaritano**, R Cons Brotero 1468, Higenópolis, T011-3824 0022. Recommended. Both have *pronto-socorro* (emergency services). Contact your consulate for names of doctors and dentists who speak your language. **Emergency and ambulance**: T192. **Fire**: T193. **Post office** Correio Central, Correios (yellow and blue signs), eg Praça do Correio, corner of Av São João and Prestes Máia, T011-3831 5222.

The coast of São Paulo

São Paulo's coast is packed at the weekend (when the city dwellers leave for the beach) and deserted during the week. There are many beautiful beaches to choose from: some backed by rainforest-covered mountains and all washed by a bottle-green warm Atlantic. The best are along the northernmost part of the state coast, the Litoral Norte, around Ubatuba, and along the Litoral Sul near Cananéia. There are beautiful offshore islands too including Brazil's largest, Ilhabela. The dividing point between the Litoral Norte and Litoral Sul is the historic city of Santos, made most famous by Pelé (there's a museum devoted to him), and dotted with a few interesting buildings and museums in a spruced-up, attractive colonial city centre.

Santos and São Vicente → *For listings, see pages 78-82. Phone code: 013.*

The Portuguese knew how to choose a location for a new settlement. **Santos** stands on an island in a bay surrounded by towering mountains and extensive areas of lowland mangrove forest – a setting equally as beautiful as that of Salvador or Rio. When it was dominated by colonial houses, churches and clean white-sand beaches Santos itself must have been one of Brazil's most enchanting cities. But in the 20th century an evil reputation for yellow fever and industrial pollution from nearby Cubatão left the city to decay and it lost much of its architecture along with its charm. Contemporary Santos, however, is getting its act together. The old colonial centre has been tidied up and Scottish trams ferry tourists past the city's sights. These include a series of colonial churches and the Bolsa do Café – a superb little museum whose café-restaurant serves the most delicious espresso in Brazil. Santos is also Pelé's home and the city where he played for almost all his career. Santos FC has a museum devoted to the club and to Pelé and it is easy to attend a game.

On the mainland, **São Vicente** is, to all intents and purposes, a suburb of Santos, having been absorbed into the conurbation. It was the first town founded in Brazil, in 1532, but nowadays it is scruffy and with very few sights of interest but for the rather dilapidated colonial church, the Matriz São Vicente Mártir (1542, rebuilt in 1757) in the Praça do Mercado. The Litoral Sul begins after São Vicente.

Arriving in Santos and São Vicente
Getting there Santos is served by regular buses from São Paulo as well as towns along the Litoral Norte and Litoral Sul, such as Curitiba, Rio de Janeiro and Florianópolis. Buses arrive at the **rodoviária** ① *Praça dos Andradas 45, T013-3219 2194*, close to the colonial centre. Those from São Paulo also stop at Ponta da Praia and José Menino, which are nearer to the main hotel district in Gonzaga. A taxi to Gonzaga from the bus station costs about US$7; all taxis have meters.

Getting around The best way to get around the centre of Santos is by the restored British 19th-century trams, which leave on guided tours (Tuesday-Sunday 1100-1700) from in front of the Prefeitura Municipal on Praça Visconde de Mauá. The tram passes most of the interesting sights, including the *azulejo*-covered houses on Rua do Comércio, the **Bolsa do Café** and some of the oldest churches. Local buses run from the colonial centre and *rodoviária* to the seafront – look for Gonzaga or Praia on their destination plaque. Bus fares within Santos are US$1.50; to São Vicente US$1.75. See www.santoscidade.com.br for further details.

Orientation The centre of the city is on the north side of the island. Due south, on the Baía de Santos, is **Gonzaga**, São Paulo's favourite beach resort where much of the city's entertainment takes place. Between these two areas, the eastern end of the island curves round within the Santos Channel. At the eastern tip, a ferry crosses the estuary to give access to the busy beaches of Guarujá and Praia Grande. The city has impressive modern buildings, wide, tree-lined avenues and wealthy suburbs.

Tourist information There are branches of **SETUR** ① *T013-3201 8000, www.santos. sp.gov.br, Mon-Fri 1000-1600, Sat 1000-1400*, at the *rodoviária*; at Praía do Gonzaga on the seafront (in a disused tram – very helpful, lots of leaflets); and next to the British-built railway station, Estação do Valongo, Largo Marquês de Monte Alegre s/n. Although poverty is apparent, the city is generally safe. However, it is wise to exercise caution at night and near the port.

Background
Santos is one of Brazil's oldest cities and has long been its most important port. The coast around the city is broken by sambaqui shell mounds that show the area has been inhabited by humans since at least 5000 BC. When the Portuguese arrived, the Tupinikin people dominated the region. However, the first settlements at neighbouring São Vicente (1532) were constantly under attack by the Tamoio who were allies of the French. The French were defeated at Rio in 1560 and the Tamoio massacred soon after.

By the 1580s Santos was a burgeoning port with some 400 houses. The first export was sugar, grown as cane at the foot of the mountains and on the plateau. By the late 19th century this had been replaced by coffee, which rapidly became Brazil's main source of income. The city was connected to São Paulo and the coffee region by the British under the guidance of Barão Visconde de Mauá, and the city grew wealthy. The seafront was lined with opulent coffee mansions and the centre was home to Brazil's most important stock exchange, the Bolsa do Café.

In the 1980s, the hinterland between the sea and mountains became the site of one of South America's most unpleasant industrial zones. The petrochemical plants of Cubatão were so notorious that they were referred to in the press as the 'The Valley of Death'. Santos and around was said to be the most contaminated corner of the planet, with so much toxic waste undermining the hills that the whole lot threatened to slip down into the sea. In the late 1980s, a spate of mutant births in Cubatão eventually prompted a clean-up operation, which is said to have been largely successful.

Places in Santos and São Vicente
The heart of the colonial centre is **Praça Mauá**. The surrounding streets are very lively in the daytime, with plenty of cheap shops and restaurants. The most interesting buildings

Santos

Centro detail

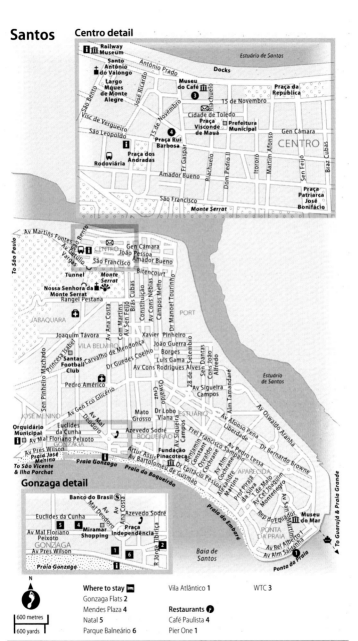

Railway Museum

Santo Antônio do Valongo

Largo Mques de Monte Alegre

Visc de Vergueiro

São Bento

São Leopoldo

José Ricardo

António Prado

Docks

Estuário de Santos

Museu do Café

15 de Novembro

Praça da República

Cidade de Toledo

Praça Visconde de Mauá

Prefeitura Municipal

Gen Câmara

CENTRO

Martim Afonso

Sen Feijó

Braz Cubas

Praça Rui Barbosa

Praça dos Andradas

Rodoviária

Ef Gaspar

Riachuelo

Amador Bueno

Dom Pedro II

Ituroro

Praça Patriarca José Bonifácio

São Francisco

Monte Serrat

Av Martins Fontes

Av Verjílio Vargas

Av Bento

CENTRO

João Pessoa

Gen Câmara

Amador Bueno

To São Paulo

São Francisco

Tunnel

Monte Serrat

Bitencourt

Nossa Senhora da Monte Serrat

Rangel Pestana

JABAQUARA

Joaquim Távora

VILA BELMIRO

Santos Football Club

Pedro Américo

Com Martins

Av Ana Costa

Bráz Cubas

Av Sen Feijó

Constituição

Av Cons Nébias

Campos Melo

Carvalho de Mendonça

Dr Guedes Coelho

Xavier Pinheiro

João Guerra Borges

Luis Gama

Av Cons Rodrigues Alves

PORT

Av Manoel Tourinho

Sen Dantas

Cons João Alfredo

28 de Setembro

Estuário de Santos

Princesa Isabel

Sen Pinheiro Machado

JOSÉ MENINO

Orquidário Municipal

Av Gen Fco Glicério

Av Mal Deodoro

Oswaldo Cruz

Estuário

Dr Lobo Viana

Mato Grosso

Dr Arthur Assis

Av Siqueira Campos

BOQUEIRÃO

Azevedo Sodré

Av Siqueira Campos

Frei Francisco Sampaio

Liberdade

Av Afonso Pena

Av Pedro Lessa

Av Oswaldo Aranha

Dr Bernardo Browne

Euclides da Cunha

Av Mal Floriano Peixoto

GONZAGA

Av Pres Wilson

Praia José Menino

To São Vicente & Ilha Porchat

Praia Gonzaga

Fundação Pinacoteca

Av Epitácio Pessoa

Av Bartolomeu de Gusmão

Praia do Boqueirão

Gonsalvi

Cochrane

Av Alm

Gothann

Av Pedro Lessa

Martins

Prof Pirajá da Silva

Alexandre

Av Cel Joaquim Montenegro

Rep do Equador

APARECIDA

Praia do Embaré

Praia do Boqueirão

Baía de Santos

PONTA DA PRAIA

Av Rei Alberto

Av Alm Saldanha

Ponta da Praia

Museu do Mar

To Guarujá & Praia Grande

Gonzaga detail

Banco do Brasil $

Euclides da Cunha

Av Mal Floriano Peixoto

GONZAGA

Av Pres Wilson

Praia Gonzaga

Av Mal Deodoro

Av Ana Costa

Azevedo Sodré

Praça Independência

Miramar Shopping

R Jorge Tibiriça

Baía de Santos

N

600 metres

600 yards

Where to stay ▨

Gonzaga Flats **2**

Mendes Plaza **4**

Natal **5**

Parque Balneário **6**

Vila Atlântico **1**

Restaurants ⚫

Café Paulista **4**

Pier One **1**

WTC **3**

are to be found here and all can be visited by tram. The most impressive is the **Museu do Café** ① *R 15 de Novembro 95, T013-3213 1750, www.museudocafe.com.br, Tue-Sat 0900-1700, Sun 1000-1700, US$2.50*, housed in the old Bolsa Oficial de Café. Its plain exterior hides a grand marble-floored art deco stock exchange and museum, with a café serving some of the best coffee and cakes in South America. The building was once open only to wealthy (and exclusively male) coffee barons who haggled beneath a magnificent stained-glass skylight, depicting a bare-breasted Brazil – the *Mãe Douro* – crowned with a star in a tropical landscape populated with tropical animals and perplexed indigenous Brazilians. The skylight and the beautiful neo-Renaissance painting of Santos that decorates the walls of the exchange is by Brazil's most respected 19th-century artist, Benedito Calixto, who was born in Santos. One of the few remaining coffee baron mansions, the **Fundação Pinacoteca** ① *Av Bartolomeu de Gusmão 15, T013-3288 2260, www.pinacotecadesantos. org.br, Tue-Sun 0900-1800, free*, on the seafront, is now a gallery housing some of his paintings, most of them landscapes, which give some idea of the city's original beauty.

Santos has a few interesting and ancient colonial churches. Only the **Santuário Santo Antônio do Valongo** ① *Marquez de Monte Alegre s/n, T013-3219 1481, www.portalvalongo. com, Tue-Sun 0800-1700, guided tours most days after 1000 in Portuguese only*, is regularly open to the public. Its twee mock-baroque interior is from the 1930s, but the far more impressive original 17th-century altarpiece sits in the Franciscan chapel to the left of the main entrance. The statue of Christ is particularly fine. Next door to the church is the British-built terminus of the now defunct Santos–São Paulo railway, which serves as a small museum. The tourist office sits above it.

On Avenida Ana Costa there is an interesting monument to commemorate the brothers Andradas, who took a leading part in the movement for Independence. There are other monuments on Praça Rui Barbosa to Bartolomeu de Gusmão, who has a claim to the world's first historically recorded airborne ascent in 1709; in the Praça da República to Brás Cubas, who founded the city in 1534; and in the Praça José Bonifácio to the soldiers of Santos who died in the Revolution of 1932.

Brazil's iconic football hero, Pelé, played for Santos for almost all his professional life, signing when he was in his teens. **Santos Football Club** ① *R Princesa Isabel 77, Vila Belmiro, T013-3257 4000, www.santosfc.com.br, Mon 1300-1900, Tue-Sun 0900-1900, US$3, for tours of the grounds call T013-3225 7989*, has an excellent museum, the **Memorial das Conquistas**, which showcases not only the career of Pelé (with his kit, boots and other assorted personal items on display), but the history of the club. Its collection of gold and silver includes several international championship trophies. Pelé still lives in the city and can sometimes be seen at matches. To get tickets to see Santos play, check the information on their website.

Monte Serrat, just south of the city centre, has at its summit a semaphore station and look-out post which reports the arrival of all ships in Santos harbour. There is also an early 20th-century casino, and a Portuguese church, **Nossa Senhora da Monte Serrat**, where the patron, Our Lady of Montserrat, is said to have performed many miracles.

The top can be reached on foot or by **funicular** ① *www.monteserrat.com.br, 4 mins, every 30 mins, US$11.50 return*. Seven shrines have been built on the way up and annual pilgrimages are made by the local people. There are fine views.

In the western district of José Menino is the **Orquidário Municipal de Santos** ① *Praça Washington, orchid garden Tue-Sun 0900-1700, bird enclosure 0800-1800, US$1.50, (bus 19, 23, 25, 52, 37 and 73)*. The flowers bloom from October to February and there is an orchid show in November. Visitors can wander among giant subtropical and tropical trees, amazing orchids and, when the aviary is open, meet macaws, toucans and parrots. The open-air cage contains hummingbirds of 20 different species and the park is a sanctuary for other birds.

Beaches

Santos has 8 km of beaches stretching round the Baía de Santos to those of São Vicente at the western end. From east to west they are: **Ponta da Praia**, below the sea wall and on the estuary, no good for bathing, but fine for watching the movements of the ships. Next are **Aparecida**, **Embaré**, **Boqueirão**, **Gonzaga** and **José Menino** (the original seaside resort for the merchants of Santos). São Vicente's beaches of **Itararé** and **Ilha Porchat** are on the island, while **Gonzaguinha** is on the mainland. The last beach is **Itaquitanduva**, which is in a military area but may be visited with authorization. In all cases, check the cleanliness of the water before venturing in (a red flag means it is too polluted for bathing).

Excursions from Santos

The small island of **Ilha Porchat** is reached by a bridge at the far end of Santos/São Vicente bay. It has beautiful views over rocky precipices, of the high seas on one side and of the city and bay on the other. At the summit is **Terraço Chopp** ① *Av Ary Barroso 274, www. terracochopp.com.br*, a restaurant with live music most evenings and great views. On summer evenings the queues can be up to four hours, but in winter, even if it may be a little chilly at night, you won't have to wait.

Litoral Norte → *For listings, see pages 78-82.*

The resorts immediately north of Santos – Guarujá, Praia Grande and Bertioga – are built up and none too clean. The landscape becomes more beautiful at Camburi, the southernmost beach of São Sebastião province, named after the historical town that sits in front of Ilhabela, an island fringed with glorious beaches. Further north, Ubatuba, borders Rio de Janeiro state and has dozens of beautiful stretches of golden sand backed by forest-covered mountains.

Camburi, Camburizinho and Maresias → *Phone code: 012.*

Beyond Boracéia are a number of beaches, including Barra do Una, Praia da Baleia and **Camburi**. The latter is the first beach in São Sebastião province and is surrounded by the Mata Atlântica forest. It has a long stretch of sand with some surf, many *pousadas* and two of the best restaurants in São Paulo state. The best place for swimming is at **Camburizinho** (though you should avoid swimming in the river which is not clean). You can walk on the Estrada do Piavu into the Mata Atlântica to see vegetation and wildlife; bathing in the streams is permitted, but use of shampoo and other chemicals is forbidden. About 5 km from Camburi is **Praia Brava**, 45 minutes' walk through the forest. The surf here is very heavy, hence the name. Camping is possible.

The road continues from Camburi, past beaches such as **Boiçucanga** (family-orientated with many *pousadas*) to **Maresias**, which is beloved of well-to-do Paulistas who come here mostly to surf. It has some chic *pousadas* and restaurants and tends to be younger and less family orientated than Camburi.

São Sebastião → *Phone code: 012. Population: 59,000.*

From Maresias it is 21 km to São Sebastião, which was once as attractive as Paraty and still retains a pretty colonial centre, albeit surrounded by an unattractive industrial hinterland.

Ferries leave from here for the 15-minute crossing to **Ilhabela** (see below), the largest offshore island in Brazil, which is shrouded in forest on its ocean side and fringed with some of São Paulo's best beaches. There are abundant borrachudo black flies on the beaches, whose bites cause immense irritation.

The city was founded at the time when Brazil's rainforest stretched all the way from the coast to the Pantanal, and all the land north to Rio de Janeiro was ruled by the indigenous Tamoio and their French allies. The settlement was initially created as an outpost of the indigenous slave trade and a port from which to dispatch armies to fight the French and claim Rio for the Portuguese crown. After this was achieved and the Tamoio had been massacred, São Sebastião grew to become one of Brazil's first sugar-exporting ports and the hinterland was covered in vast fields of cane tilled by the enslaved indigenous Brazilians. When the number of local slaves became depleted by the lash and disease, the city became one of the first ports of the African slave trade.

Arriving in São Sebastião São Sebastião is served by regular buses from Ubatuba and Santos and is also connected to São Paulo. Ferries (for cars as well as passengers), US$2.50 per car, from Ilhabela run every 30 minutes 0600-2400 and every hour 2400-0600 (see page 81) and take 15 minutes. The **tourist office** ① *Av Altino Arantes 154, T012-3892 5323, www.saosebastiao.sp.gov.br, daily 1000-1700*, is on the waterfront one block towards the sea from Praça Major João Fernandes. Staff are very helpful and can provide maps and information on ferries to Ilhabela and beaches in the entire São Sebatstião province. The city is far cheaper for accommodation than Ilhabela.

Places São Sebastião São Sebastião's remaining colonial streets are in the few blocks between the shoreline and the Praça Major João Fernandes, which is dominated by the **Igreja Matriz** ① *daily 0900-1800*. Although this retains remnants of its original 17th-century design, this is predominantly a 19th-century reconstruction devoid of much of its original church art. However, the newly refurbished **Museu de Arte Sacra** ① *1 block south of the praça, R Sebastião Neves 90, T012-3892 4286, daily 1300-1700, free*, in the 17th-century chapel of São Gonçalo, preserves a number of 16th-century statues found in cavities in the wall of the Igreja Matriz during its restoration in 2003.

The city has a few sleepy streets of Portuguese houses, fanning out from the square, and a handful of civic buildings worth a quick look before the ferry leaves for Ilhabela. The most impressive is the **Casa Esperança** ① *Av Altino Arantes 154, now housing the offices of the Secretaria do Turismo*, on the waterfront. It was built from stone and wattle and daub glued together with whale oil, and then whitewashed with lime from thousands of crushed shells from the beaches of Ilhabela. The interior has some peeling 17th-century ceiling paintings.

Ilhabela (Ilha de São Sebastião) → *Phone code: 012. Population: 21,000 (100,000 high season).*
Ilhabela is Brazil's largest oceanic island and one of its prettiest. It is wild enough to be home to ocelots, and the lush forests on its ocean side (80% of which are protected by a state park) drip with waterfalls and are fringed with glorious beaches. Its centre is crowned with craggy peaks, often obscured by mist: **Morro de São Sebastião** (1379 m), **Morro do Papagaio** (1309 m), **Ramalho** (1285 m) and **Pico Baepi** (1025 m). Rainfall on the island is heavy, about 3000 mm a year, and there are many small biting black flies known locally as *borrachudos* – a sign that the streams on the island are unpolluted (black fly can only breed in completely unpolluted water), but a real pest.

The island is considered to be one of Brazil's sailing capitals because its 150 km of coastline offers all types of conditions. The sheltered waters of the strait are where many sailors learn their skills and the bays around the coast provide safe anchorages. There are, however, numerous tales of shipwrecks because of the unpredictable winds, sudden mists and strange forces playing havoc with compasses, but these provide plenty of adventure for divers. There are over 30 wrecks that can be dived, the most notable being the *Príncipe de Asturias*, a transatlantic liner that went down off the Ponta de Pirabura in 1916.

Arriving in Ilhabela There are good transport connections with the mainland via São Sebastião. Ferries run day and night and leave regularly from the São Sebastião waterfront, taking about 20 minutes; free for pedestrians, cars US$2.50. It is very difficult to find space for a car on the ferry during summer weekends. A bus meets the ferry and runs to Ilhabela town and along the west coast. Try to visit during the week when the island feels deserted, and avoid high season (December to February). Hotels and *pousadas* are expensive; many budget travellers choose to stay in São Sebastião instead. For information contact the **Secretaria de Turismo** ① *Praça Ver, José Leite dos Passos 14, Barra Velha, T012-3895 7220, www.ilhabela.com.br.* ▸▸ *See Transport, page 81.*

Places in Ilhabela Most of the island's residents live on the sheltered shore facing the mainland, along which are a number of upmarket *pousadas*. Swimming is not recommended on this side of the island within 4 km of São Sebastião because of pollution. Watch out for oil, sandflies and jellyfish on the sand and in the water.

About 20 minutes north of the ferry terminal is the main population centre, **Vila Ilhabela**. The village has some pretty colonial buildings and the parish church, **Nossa Senhora da Ajuda e Bom Sucesso**, dates from the 17th century and has been restored. There are restaurants, cafés and shops. Four kilometres north of Ilhabela, **Pedras do Sino** (Bell Rocks) are curious seashore boulders which, when struck with a piece of iron or stone, emit a loud bell-like note. There is a beach here and a campsite nearby.

From Vila Ilhabela, the road hugs the coast, sometimes high above the sea, towards the south of the island. An old *fazenda*, **Engenho d'Água**, a few kilometres from town in a grand 18th-century mansion (not open to the public), gives its name to one of the busiest beaches. About 10 km further, you can visit the old **Feiticeira** plantation. It has underground dungeons, and can be reached by bus, taxi, or horse and buggy. A trail leads down from the plantation to the beautiful beach of the same name.

On the south coast is the fishing village of **Bonete**, which has 500 m of beach and can be reached either by boat (1½ hours), or by driving to Borrifos at the end of the road, then walking along a rainforest-covered trail for three hours – a beautiful walk.

Much of the Atlantic side of the island is protected by the **Parque Estadual de Ilhabela**. There is a dirt road across to the east of the island, but it requires a 4WD. A few kilometres along this road is a turning to the terraced waterfall of **Cachoeira da Toca** (US$4). Set in dense jungle close to the foot of the Baepi peak, the cool freshwater pools are good for bathing and attract lots of butterflies. The locals claim that there are more than 300 waterfalls on the island, but only a few of them can be reached on foot; those that can are worth the effort. There is a 50-km return trek from Vila Ilhabela over the hump of the island down towards the Atlantic. The route follows part of the old slave trail and requires a local guide as it negotiates dense tropical forest. It takes at least two days.

Some of the island's best beaches are on the Atlantic side of the island and can only be reached by boat. **Praia dos Castelhanos** is recommended. At the cove of **Saco do Sombrio**

English, Dutch and French pirates sheltered in the 16th and 17th centuries. Needless to say, this has led to legends of hidden treasure, but the most potent story about the place is that of the Englishman, Thomas Cavendish. In 1592 he sacked Santos and set it on fire. He then sailed to Saco do Sombrio where his crew mutinied, hanged Cavendish, sank their boats and settled on the island.

Ubatuba → *For listings, see pages 78-82. Phone code: 012. Population: 67,000.*

This is one of the most beautiful stretches of the São Paulo coast and has been recognized as such by the local tourist industry for many years. In all, there are 72 beaches of varying sizes, some in coves, some on islands. Surfing is the main pastime, of which it is said to be capital, but there is a whole range of watersports on offer, including sailing to and around the offshore islands. The **Tropic of Capricorn** runs through the beach of Itaguá, just south of the town.

The commercial centre of Ubatuba is at the northern end of the bay by the estuary, by which the fishing boats enter and leave. A bridge crosses the estuary, giving access to the coast north of town. A small jetty with a lighthouse at the end protects the river mouth and this is a pleasant place to watch the boats come and go. The seafront, stretching south from the jetty, is built up along its length, but there are hardly any high-rise blocks. In the commercial centre are shops, banks, services, lots of restaurants (most serving pizza and fish), but few hotels. These are mainly found on the beaches north and south and can be reached from the Costamar bus terminal.

Arriving in Ubatuba
The road from São Sebastião is paved, so a journey from São Paulo along the coast is possible. Ubatuba is 70 km from Paraty. There are regular buses from São Paulo, São José dos Campos, Paraibuna, Caraguatatuba, Paraty and Rio de Janeiro. The beaches are spread out over a wide area, so if you are staying in Ubatuba town and don't have a car, you will need to take one of the frequent buses. Taxis in town can be very expensive. ▸▸ *See Transport, page 81.*

The **tourist office** ⓘ *R Guarani 465, T012-3833 9007, www.ubatuba.sp.gov.br*, is on the seafront. The area gets very crowded at carnival time as Cariocas come to escape the crowds in Rio. There is a small airport from which stunt fliers take off to wheel over the bay. In summer 10-minute panoramic flights and helicopter rides over Ubatuba are offered from here from around US$75.

Places in Ubatuba
Ubatuba has a few historic buildings, such as the **Igreja da Matriz** on Praça da Matriz, dating back to the 18th century. It has only one tower, the old 19th-century prison, which now houses the small historical museum. Other interesting buildings include: **Cadeia Velha** on Praça Nóbrega; the 18th-century **Câmara Municipal** on Avenida Iperoig; and the **Sobrado do Porto**, the 19th-century customs house at Praça Anchieta 38, which contains **Fundart** (the Art and Culture Foundation). Mostly, though, it is a modern, functional town. In the surrounding countryside there are *fazendas* which are often incorporated into the *trilhas ecológicas* (nature trails) along the coast.

The **Projeto Tamar** ⓘ *R Antonio Athanasio da Silva 273, Itaguá, T012-3432 6202, www.ubatuba.com.br/tamar*, is a branch of the national project which studies and preserves marine turtles. The **Aquário de Ubatuba** ⓘ *R Guarani 859, T012-3432 1382, www.aquariodeubatuba.com.br, Fri-Sat 1000-2200, Sun-Thu 1000-2000, US$9, children half-price,* has well-displayed Amazon and Pantanal species including caimans and piranhas and some reef fish, including Brazilian batfish (*Ogocephalus vespertilio*), long-spined porcupine fish (*Diodon holocanthus*) and dusky grouper (*Epinephelus marginatus*). Not all of the species are Brazilian eg the leopard sharks (from the Pacific).

Beaches

The only place where swimming is definitely not recommended is near the town's sewage outflow between Praia do Cruzeiro and Praia Itaguá. The sand and water close to the jetty don't look too inviting either. The most popular beaches are **Praia Tenório**, **Praia Grande** and **Praia Toninhas** (4.5 km, 6 km and 8 km south respectively). Condominiums, apartments, hotels and *pousadas* line these beaches on both sides of the coast road. Of the municipality's 72 beaches, those to the south are the more developed although the further you go from town in either direction, the less built up they are. Boogie boards can be hired at many of the beaches, or you can buy your own in town for around US$5.

Saco da Ribeira, 13 km south, is a natural harbour that has been made into a yacht marina. Schooners leave from here for excursions to **Ilha Anchieta** (or dos Porcos), a popular four-hour trip. On the island are beaches, trails and a prison, which was in commission from 1908 to 1952. The **Costamar** bus from Ubatuba to Saco da Ribeira runs every half an hour (US$0.85) and will drop you at the turning by the **Restaurante Pizzeria Malibu**. It's a short walk to the docks and boatyards where an unsealed road leads to the right, through the boatyards, to a track along the shore. It ends at the **Praia da Ribeira** from where you can follow the track round a headland to the beaches of **Flamengo**, **Flamenguinho** and **Sete Fontes**. It's a pleasant stroll (about one hour to Flamengo), but there is no shade and you need to take water. Note the sign before Flamengo on one of the private properties: "*Propriedade particular. Cuidado com elefante*"!

The coast of São Paulo listings

For hotel and restaurant price codes and other relevant information, see pages 8-11.

🛏 Where to stay

Santos *p69, map p71*

Discounts of up to 50% are available during low season. There are many cheap hotels near the Orquidário Municipal a few blocks from the beach.

$$$$ Mendes Plaza, Av Floriano Peixoto 42, a block from the beach in the main shopping area, T013-3208 6400, www.mendeshoteis.com.br. A large, newly refurbished, 1970s business-orientated hotel with 2 restaurants and a rooftop pool.

$$$$ Parque Balneário Hotel, Av Ana Costa 555, Gonzaga, T013-3289 5700, www.parquebalneario.com.br. The city's 5-star hotel, with newly refurbished rooms, full business facilities and a rooftop pool overlooking the beach. Close to the shops and restaurants.

$$$ Ville Atlântico Hotel, Av Pres Wilson 1, T013-3289 4500, www.atlantico-hotel.com.br. A/c rooms in a newly renovated, well-kept 1930s hotel on the seafront. All rooms have TV; the best are in the upper floors with sea views. There's a decent business centre, sauna, bar and restaurant. There are number of other hotels in Santos in the same group.

$$ Gonzaga Flats, R Jorge Tibiriçá 41, Gonzaga, T013-3289 5800, www.gonzaga flat.tur.br. Apartments in a 1990s block, all with kitchenettes and small sitting rooms with sofa beds. Space for up to 4 people.

$$ Hotel Natal, Av Mal Floriano Peixoto 104, Gonzaga T013-3284 2732, www.hotelnatal.com.br. Fan-cooled or a/c apartments with or without bathrooms. Cable TV.

Camburi, Camburizinho and Maresias *p73*

$$$ Camburyzinho, Estr Camburi 200, Km 41, Camburizinho, T012-3865 2625,

www.pousadacamburizinho.com.br. 30 smart rooms in mock-colonial annexes gathered around a pool, with a bar and beach service.

$$ Pousada das Praias, R Piauí 70, Camburizinho, T012-3865 1474, www.pousadadaspraias.com.br. A lovely beachside *pousada* in tropical gardens, with annexes of thatched-roof wooden rooms with large glass windows and terraces overlooking a pool and sauna. The *pousada* contributes part of its profits to the local community.

$$ Toca da Praia, Av Paquetá 423, Maresias, T012-3865 6667, www.tocada praia.com.br. Family-friendly pousada with a pool for adults and kids, a/c rooms and a generous breakfast.

São Sebastião *p73*

The city itself is not particularly desirable so only stay here if you have to, otherwise it's best to head for Ilhabela or further along the coast. There are a few cheap places near the main *praça* and *rodoviária*. See www.guiapousadas.com.br for more options along the São Sebastião coast.

$$ Roma, Praça João Fernandes 174, São Sebastião city, T012-3892 1016, www.hotelroma.tur.br. Simple but well-maintained rooms around a fig-tree filled courtyard. The simplest are a little scruffy. Includes breakfast.

Ilhabela *p74*

There are a number of moderate and cheap hotels on the road to the left of the ferry.

$$$$ Barulho d'Agua, R Manoel Pombo 250, Curral, Km 14, T012-3894 2021, www.barulhodagua.com.br. Intimate little cabins with thatched roofs and rustic, chunky wood furniture set in rainforest next to a clear river. Very romantic and with a good restaurant.

$$$$ Maison Joly, R Antonio Lisboa Alves 278, Morro do Cantagalo, T012-3896 1201, www.maisonjoly.com.br. Exquisite little *pousada* perfect for couples. Each cabin is tastefully decorated in its own style and has a wonderful view out over the bay. Great restaurant and pool. Private, intimate and quiet. No children allowed.

$$$ Ilhabela, Av Pedro Paulo de Morais 151, Saco da Capela, T012-3896 1083, www.hotel ilhabela.com.br. One of the larger *pousadas*, orientated to families and with a well-equipped but small gym, pool, restaurant and bar and good breakfast. Recommended.

$$$ Porto Pousada Saco da Capela, R Itapema 167, T012-3896 8020, www. sacodacapela.com.br. 18 carefully decorated cabins set in a rocky forest garden on a steep hill. Good pool and breakfast.

$$ Canto Bravo, Praia do Bonete, T012-9766 0478, www.pousadacantobravo.com. br. Set on a secluded beach 1½ hrs' walk (or 20-min boat ride) from Ponta de Sepituba. Modest and elegantly decorated cabins and excellent simple breakfast and lunch (included in the price).

$$ Ilhabela, R Benedito Serafim Sampaio 371, Pereque, T012-3896 2725, www. bonnsventoshostel.com.br. A well-kept and well-run mock-colonial hostel with terracotta tiled roofs and solid wooden and wicker furniture in smart, airy public areas. Dorms are stark and simple with little more than beds and lockers. Suites are more spacious and brighter, with metal tables outside and en suite bathrooms. The hostel has a pool, a large garden and sits a short walk from the beach.

$$ Pousada dos Hibiscos, Av Pedro Paulo de Morais 714, T012-3896 1375, www. pousadadoshibiscos.com.br. Little group of cabins set around a pool with a sauna, gym and bar. Nice atmosphere. Recommended.

$$ Tamara, R Jacob Eduardo Toedtli 163, Itaquanduba, T012-3896 2543, www. pousada-tamara.com.br. 17 *cabañas* with a/c around a small pool.

$$ Vila das Pedra, R Antenor Custodio da Silva 46, Cocaia, T012-3896 2433, www.viladaspedras.com.br. 11 chalets in a forest garden. Tastefully decorated and a nice pool.

Ubatuba *p76*
Very cheap accommodation is hard to come by and at all holiday times no hotel charges less than US$40.

$$ São Charbel, Praça Nóbrega 280, T012-3832 1090, www.saocharbel.com. br. Plain white a/c rooms with floor tiles, double beds with fitted bedside tables and Brazilian TV. The hotel sits on the busy main square. The advertised rooftop 'pool' is, in reality, a tiny plunge pool.

$$ São Nicolau, R Conceição 213, T012-3832 5007, www.hotelsaonicolau.com. br. Very simple a/c rooms sitting over a colourful restaurant, a 3-min walk from the bus station. The *pousada* is convenient for the town beach restaurants and services. Friendly and well looked after, with a good breakfast.

$$ Xaréu, R Jordão Homem da Costa 413, T012-3832 1525, www.hotelxareubatuba. com.br. 3-min walk from the bus station, convenient for the town beach restaurants and services. Pretty rooms with wrought-iron balconies in a pleasant garden area. Good value, excellent breakfast.

Beach hotels
$$$$ Recanto das Toninhas, Praia das Toninhas, T012-3842 1410, www.toninhas. com.br. Part of the **Roteiros de Charme** group (see page 9). Elegant *cabañas* and suites of rooms in a large thatched-roofed building. The best with have sea views and are set around a pretty pool with a full range of services and activities, including a sauna, restaurant, bar, tennis court and excursions.

$$$ Refúgio do Corsário, Baia Fortaleza, 25 km south of Ubatuba, T012-3443 9148, www.corsario.com.br. A clean, quiet hotel on the waterfront with a large pool set on a palm-shaded lawn overlooking the ocean.

$$$ Saveiros, R Laranjeira 227, Praia do Lázaro, 14 km from town, T012-3842 0172, www.hotelsaveiros.com.br. Pretty little *pousada* with a pool and a decent restaurant. English spoken.

$$$ Solar das Águas Cantantes,
Estr Saco da Ribeira 253, Praia do
Lázaro, Km 14, T012-3842 0178, www.
solardasaguascantantes.com.br. A mock-
Portuguese colonial house replete with
azulejos and set in a shady tropical garden.
The restaurant is one of the best on the
São Paulo coast and serves excellent
seafood and Bahian dishes.

$$ Rosa Penteado, Av Beira-Mar 183,
Praia de Picinguaba, T012-3836 9119,
www.pousadarosapicinguaba.com.br. 4
pretty beachside *cabañas* decorated with
paintings and objects made by the owner.
The price includes a very good breakfast
and dinner.

$ Tribo Hostel, R Amoreira 71, Praia do
Lázaro, 14 km from Ubatuba, T012-
3432 0585, www.ubatubahostel.com.
Great-value hostel on one of the prettiest
beaches in Ubatuba. Simple tiled dorms
and doubles, all fan-cooled and with
shared bathrooms.

● Restaurants

Santos *p69, map p71*
$$ Pier One, Av Almirante Saldanha
da Gama, Ponta da Praia. Good evening
option in a restaurant perched over the
water next to the Ponte Edgard Perdigao
bridge. Very good *meca santista* (a local fish
speciality served with banana, manioc flour
and bacon) and live music at weekends.
$$ WTC, R 15 de Novembro 111/113,
Centro Histórico, T013-3219 7175. A
businessman's club housed in a handsome
19th-century building. Popular with local
bigwigs. One of the best restaurants
in the city with a Mediterranean-
influenced menu.
$ Café Paulista, Praça Rui Barbosa 8 at
R do Comércio, Centro Histórico, T013-
3219 5550. A Santos institution. Founded
in 1911 by Italians, this place has long been
serving great Portuguese dishes such as
bacalhau, and bar snacks (such as *empada
camarão*), and coffee.

**Camburi, Camburizinho and
Maresias** *p73*
There are numerous cheap and mid-range
restaurants with bars and nightclubs along
the São Sebastião coast and some excellent
restaurants around Camburizinho.
$$$ Acqua, R Estr Do Camburi 2000,
Camburizinho, T012-3865 1866. Superb
food with a view out over Camburi and
Praia de Baleia beach. Come for a sunset
cocktail and then dine by candlelight.
$$$ Manacá, R do Manacá, Camburizinho,
T012-3865 1566. Closed Mon and Wed.
One of the best restaurants on the São
Paulo coast, romantic setting, in a rainforest
garden reached by a candlelit boardwalk.
Come for dinner. Worth a special trip.

Ilhabela *p74*
There are cheap places in the town,
including a *padaria* (bakery) and snack bars.
$$$ Pizzabela, Hotel Ilha Deck, Av
Alm Tamandaré 805, Itaguassu, T012-
3896 1489. Paulistanos consider their
pizza the best in the world. This is one
of the few restaurants outside the city
serving pizza, São Paulo-style. Expect
lots of cheese. Nice surrounds.
$$$ Viana, Av Leonardo Reale 1560, Praia
do Viana, T012-3896 1089. The best and
most expensive restaurant on the island,
with excellent seafood and light Italian
dishes. Good wine list. Book ahead.

Ubatuba *p76*
There is a string of mid-range restaurants
along the seafront on Av Iperoig, as far
as the roundabout by the airport.
$$$ Giorgio, Av Leovigildo Dias
Vieira 248, Itaguá. Sophisticated
Italian restaurant/bar.
$$$ Solar das Águas Cantantes, (see
Where to stay). Very good seafood and
Bahian restaurant in elegant surrounds.
$$ Pizzeria São Paulo, Praça da Paz
de Iperoig 26. Undeniably chic gourmet
pizzeria in beautifully restored building.
Owned by a young lawyer who brings

The biggest rodeo in the world

The world's biggest annual rodeo, the Festa do Peão Boiadeiro, is held during the third week in August in Barretos, some 115 km northwest of Ribeirão Preto. The town is completely taken over as up to a million fans come to watch the horsemanship, enjoy the concerts, eat, drink and shop in what has become the epitome of Brazilian cowboy culture. There are over 1000 rodeos a year in Brazil, but this is the ultimate. The stadium, which has a capacity for 35,000 people, was designed by Oscar Niemeyer and the wind funnels through the middle, cool the competitors and the spectators. Since the 1950s, when Barretos' rodeo began, the event grew slowly until the mid-1980s when it really took off. Tours from the UK are run by **Last Frontiers**, www.lastfrontiers.co.uk.

the authentic Italian ingredients for the gorgeous pizzas from São Paulo every weekend.
$$ Senzala, Av Iperoig. Established 30 years ago, this Italian has a great atmosphere. Don't miss the seafood spaghetti. Recommended.

⊖ Transport

Santos *p69, map p71*
Bus To **São Vicente**, US$1.50. For most suburbs buses leave from Praça Mauá, in the centre of the city. Heading south, several daily buses connect Santos to **Peruíbe**, **Iguape** and **Cananéia** for **Ilha Comprida** and **Ilha do Cardoso**.
   There are buses to **São Paulo** (80 mins, US$10) approximately every 15 mins, from the *rodoviária* near the city centre, José Menino or Ponta da Praia (opposite the ferry to Guarujá). Note that the 2 highways between São Paulo and Santos are sometimes very crowded, especially at rush hours and weekends. To **Guarulhos/Cumbica airports**, 11 buses a day, US$10, allow plenty of time as the bus goes through Guarulhos, 2 hrs. To **Rio de Janeiro**, numerous daily, 8 hrs, US$57.50. 6 daily for **São Sebastião** (US$22, change buses if necessary), 6 daily **Caraguatatuba** (US$25). For **Ubatuba** and **Paraty** change at Caraguatatuba.

Taxi All taxis have meters. The fare from Gonzaga to the bus station is about US$15. Cooper Rádio Táxi, T013-3232 7177.

São Sebastião *p73*
Bus 2 buses a day to **Rio de Janeiro** with Normandy, 0830 and 2300 (plus 1630 on Fri and Sun), can be heavily booked in advance, US$30 (US$10 from Paraty) 6½ hrs; 12 a day to **Santos**, via Guarujá, 4 hrs, US$11; 11 buses a day also to **São Paulo**, US$15, which run inland via **São José dos Campos**, unless you ask for the service via **Bertioga**, only 2 a day. Other buses run along the coast via **Maresias**, **Camburi** or north through **Ubatuba**. Last bus leaves at 2200.
Ferry Free ferry to **Ilhabela** for foot passengers, see below.

Ilhabela *p74*
Bus A bus runs along the coastal strip facing the mainland. Litorânea runs buses from Ilhabela town through to **São Paulo** (office at R Dr Carvalho 136) but it is easiest to reach the island by taking a bus from São Paulo to São Sebastião across the water and then the ferry across to Ilhabela.

Ferry The 15- to 20-min ferry to **São Sebastião** runs non-stop day and night. Free for foot passengers; cars cost US$1 weekdays, US$10 at weekends.

Ubatuba *p76*

Bus· There are 3 bus terminals.
Rodoviária Costamar, R Hans Staden and R Conceição, serves all local destinations.

The *rodoviária* at R Prof Thomaz Galhardo 513, for **São José** buses to **Paraty**, US$7.50, 45 mins; to **Rio de Janeiro**, 8 daily, US$35, 5 hrs; and **São Paulo**, 17 daily, US$27.50, 4 hrs. Frequent services to **Caraguatatuba** (change here for São Sebastião and Santos).

Rodoviária Litorânea is the main bus station. To get there, go up Conceição for 8 blocks from Praça 13 de Maio, turn right on R Rio Grande do Sul, then left into R Dra Maria V Jean.

❶ Directory

Santos *p69, map p71*
Banks Open 1000-1730. ATMs in Santos are very unreliable and often out of order. Visa ATMs at **Banco do Brasil**, R 15 de Novembro 195, Centro and Av Ana Costa, Gonzaga. Many others.

Ilhabela *p74*
Banks Bradesco, Praça Col Julião M Negrão 29 in Vila Ilhabela.

Ubatuba *p76*
Banks There is a Banco 24 Horas next to the tourist office and an **HSBC** ATM at 85 R Conceição. The **Banco do Brasil** in Praça Nóbrega does not have ATMs.

Contents

Footnotes

Basic Portuguese for travellers

Learning Portuguese is a useful part of the preparation for a trip to Brazil and no volume of dictionaries, phrase books or word lists will provide the same enjoyment as being able to communicate directly with the people of the country you are visiting. It is a good idea to make an effort to grasp the basics before you go. As you travel you will pick up more of the language and the more you know, the more you will benefit from your stay.

General pronunciation
Within Brazil itself, there are variations in pronunciation, intonation, phraseology and slang. This makes for great richness and for the possibility of great enjoyment in the language. A couple of points which the newcomer to the language will spot immediately are the use of the tilde (~) over 'a' and 'o'. This makes the vowel nasal, as does a word ending in 'm' or 'ns', or a vowel followed by 'm' + consonant, or by 'n' + consonant. Another important point of spelling is that for words ending in 'i' and 'u' the emphasis is on the last syllable, though (unlike Spanish) no accent is used. This is especially relevant in place names like Buriti, Guarapari, Caxambu, Iguaçu. Note also the use of 'ç', which changes the pronunciation of c from hard [k] to soft [s].

Personal pronouns
In conversation, most people refer to 'you' as *você*, although in the south and in Pará *tu* is more common. To be more polite, use *O Senhor/A Senhora*. For 'us', *gente* (people, folks) is very common when it includes you too.

Portuguese words and phrases

Greetings and courtesies

hello	*oi*	how are you?	*como vai você tudo bem?/tudo bom?*
good morning	*bom dia*		
good afternoon	*boa tarde*	I am fine	*vou bem/tudo bem*
good evening/night	*boa noite*	pleased to meet you	*um prazer*
goodbye	*adeus/tchau*	no	*não*
see you later	*até logo*	yes	*sim*
please	*por favor/faz favor*	excuse me	*com licença*
thank you	*obrigado* (if a man is speaking)/ *obrigada* (if a woman is speaking)	I don't understand	*não entendo*
		please speak slowly	*fale devagar por favor*
		what is your name?	*qual é seu nome?*
		my name is …	*o meu nome é …*
thank you very much	*muito obrigado/ muito obrigada*	go away!	*vai embora!*

Basic questions

where is?	*onde está/ onde fica?*	when?	*quando?*
why?	*por que?*	I want to go to …	*quero ir para …*
how much does it cost?	*quanto custa?*	when does the bus leave?/arrive?	*a que hor sai/ chega o ônibus?*
what for?	*para que?*	is this the way to the church?	*aquí é o caminho para a igreja?*
how much is it?	*quanto é?*		
how do I get to … ?	*para chegar a … ?*		

Basics

bathroom/toilet	*banheiro*	notes/coins	*notas/moedas*
police (policeman)	*a polícia (o polícia)*	cash	*dinheiro*
hotel	*o (a pensão, a hospedaria)*	breakfast	*o caféde manh*
		lunch	*o almoço*
restaurant	*o restaurante (o lanchonete)*	dinner/supper	*o jantar*
		meal	*a refeição*
post office	*o correio*	drink	*a bebida*
telephone office	*(central) telefônica*	mineral water	*a água mineral*
supermarket	*o supermercado*	soft fizzy drink	*o refrigerante*
market	*o mercado*	beer	*a cerveja*
bank	*o banco*	without sugar	*sem açúcar*
bureau de change	*a casa de câmbio*	without meat	*sem carne*
exchange rate	*a taxa de câmbio*		

Getting around

on the left/right	*à esquerda/ à direita*	flight	*o vôa*
		first/second class	*primeira/ segunda clase*
straight on	*direto*		
to walk	*caminhar*	train station	*a ferroviária*
bus station	*a rodoviária*	combined bus and train station	*a rodoferroviária*
bus	*o ônibus*		
bus stop	*a parada*	ticket	*o passagem/ o bilhete*
train	*a trem*		
airport	*o aeroport*	ticket office	*a bilheteria*
aeroplane/airplane	*o avião*		

Accommodation

room	*quarto*	hot/cold water	*água quente/fria*
noisy	*barulhento*	to make up/clean	*limpar*
single/double room	*(quarto de) solteiro/ (quarto para) casal*	sheet(s)	*o lençol (os lençóis)*
		blankets	*as mantas*
room with two beds	*quarto com duas camas*	pillow	*o travesseiro*
		clean/dirty towels	*as toalhas limpas/ sujas*
with private bathroom	*quarto com banheiro*	toilet paper	*o papel higiêico*

Index

Titles available in the Footprint *Focus* range

Latin America	UK RRP	US RRP
Bahia & Salvador	£7.99	$11.95
Brazilian Amazon	£7.99	$11.95
Brazilian Pantanal	£6.99	$9.95
Buenos Aires & Pampas	£7.99	$11.95
Cartagena & Caribbean Coast	£7.99	$11.95
Costa Rica	£8.99	$12.95
Cuzco, La Paz & Lake Titicaca	£8.99	$12.95
El Salvador	£5.99	$8.95
Guadalajara & Pacific Coast	£6.99	$9.95
Guatemala	£8.99	$12.95
Guyana, Guyane & Suriname	£5.99	$8.95
Havana	£6.99	$9.95
Honduras	£7.99	$11.95
Nicaragua	£7.99	$11.95
Northeast Argentina & Uruguay	£8.99	$12.95
Paraguay	£5.99	$8.95
Quito & Galápagos Islands	£7.99	$11.95
Recife & Northeast Brazil	£7.99	$11.95
Rio de Janeiro	£8.99	$12.95
São Paulo	£5.99	$8.95
Uruguay	£6.99	$9.95
Venezuela	£8.99	$12.95
Yucatán Peninsula	£6.99	$9.95

Asia	UK RRP	US RRP
Angkor Wat	£5.99	$8.95
Bali & Lombok	£8.99	$12.95
Chennai & Tamil Nadu	£8.99	$12.95
Chiang Mai & Northern Thailand	£7.99	$11.95
Goa	£6.99	$9.95
Gulf of Thailand	£8.99	$12.95
Hanoi & Northern Vietnam	£8.99	$12.95
Ho Chi Minh City & Mekong Delta	£7.99	$11.95
Java	£7.99	$11.95
Kerala	£7.99	$11.95
Kolkata & West Bengal	£5.99	$8.95
Mumbai & Gujarat	£8.99	$12.95

Africa & Middle East	UK RRP	US RRP
Beirut	£6.99	$9.95
Cairo & Nile Delta	£8.99	$12.95
Damascus	£5.99	$8.95
Durban & KwaZulu Natal	£8.99	$12.95
Fès & Northern Morocco	£8.99	$12.95
Jerusalem	£8.99	$12.95
Johannesburg & Kruger National Park	£7.99	$11.95
Kenya's Beaches	£8.99	$12.95
Kilimanjaro & Northern Tanzania	£8.99	$12.95
Luxor to Aswan	£8.99	$12.95
Nairobi & Rift Valley	£7.99	$11.95
Red Sea & Sinai	£7.99	$11.95
Zanzibar & Pemba	£7.99	$11.95

Europe	UK RRP	US RRP
Bilbao & Basque Region	£6.99	$9.95
Brittany West Coast	£7.99	$11.95
Cádiz & Costa de la Luz	£6.99	$9.95
Granada & Sierra Nevada	£6.99	$9.95
Languedoc: Carcassonne to Montpellier	£7.99	$11.95
Málaga	£5.99	$8.95
Marseille & Western Provence	£7.99	$11.95
Orkney & Shetland Islands	£5.99	$8.95
Santander & Picos de Europa	£7.99	$11.95
Sardinia: Alghero & the North	£7.99	$11.95
Sardinia: Cagliari & the South	£7.99	$11.95
Seville	£5.99	$8.95
Sicily: Palermo & the Northwest	£7.99	$11.95
Sicily: Catania & the Southeast	£7.99	$11.95
Siena & Southern Tuscany	£7.99	$11.95
Sorrento, Capri & Amalfi Coast	£6.99	$9.95
Skye & Outer Hebrides	£6.99	$9.95
Verona & Lake Garda	£7.99	$11.95

North America	UK RRP	US RRP
Vancouver & Rockies	£8.99	$12.95

Australasia	UK RRP	US RRP
Brisbane & Queensland	£8.99	$12.95
Perth	£7.99	$11.95

For the latest books, e-books and a wealth of travel information, visit us at:
www.footprinttravelguides.com.

footprinttravelguides.com

Join us on facebook for the latest travel news, product releases, offers and amazing competitions:
www.facebook.com/footprintbooks.